DYNAMITE ENTERTAINMENT PROUDLY PRESENTS

CHARLAINE HARRIS
GRAVE SIGHT
BOOK THREE

DYNAMITE ENTERTAINMENT PROUDLY PRESENTS

CHARLAINE HARRIS
GRAVE SIGHT
BOOK THREE

written by CHARLAINE HARRIS & WILLIAM HARMS
art by DENIS MEDRI
colors by PAOLO FRANCESCUTTO Gotem Studio
letters by BILL TORTOLINI
cover by BENOIT SPRINGER

contributing editor RICH YOUNG
consultation ERNST DABEL & LES DABEL
special thanks to JOSHUA BILMES

ISBN10: 1-60690-269-5
ISBN13: 978-1-60690-269-1

10 9 8 7 6 5 4 3 2

Dynamite Entertainment:

NICK BARRUCCI · PRESIDENT
JUAN COLLADO · CHIEF OPERATING OFFICER
JOSEPH RYBANDT · EDITOR
JOSH JOHNSON · CREATIVE DIRECTOR
RICH YOUNG · BUSINESS DEVELOPMENT
JASON ULLMEYER · SENIOR DESIGNER
JOSH JOHNSON · TRAFFIC COORDINATOR
CHRIS CANIANO · PRODUCTION ASSISTANT

WWW.DYNAMITE.NET

For media rights, foreign rights, promotions, licensing, and advertising: **marketing@dynamite.net**

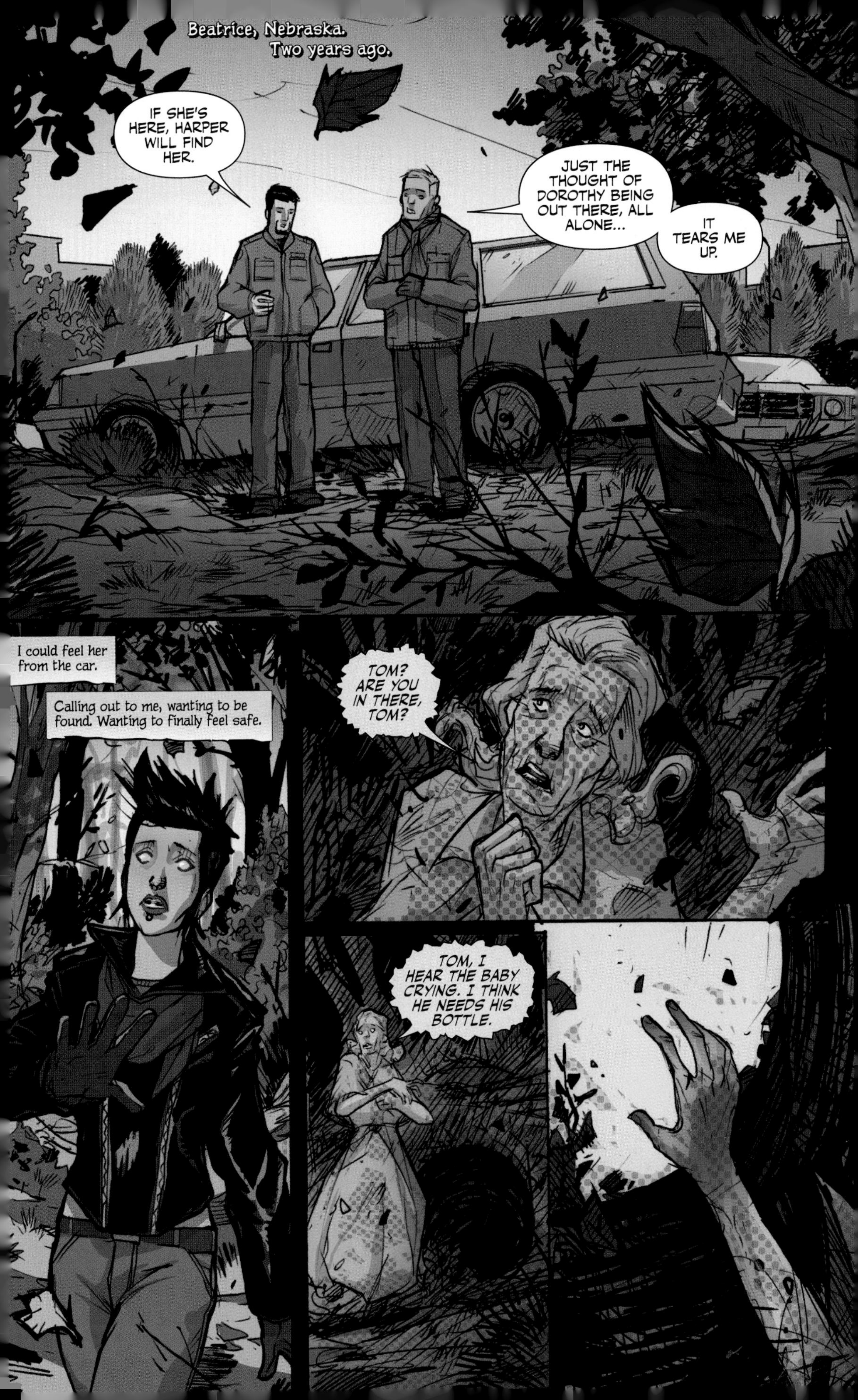

Beatrice, Nebraska.
Two years ago.
IF SHE'S HERE, HARPER WILL FIND HER.
JUST THE THOUGHT OF DOROTHY BEING OUT THERE, ALL ALONE...
IT TEARS ME UP.
I could feel her from the car.
Calling out to me, wanting to be found. Wanting to finally feel safe.
TOM? ARE YOU IN THERE, TOM?
TOM, I HEAR THE BABY CRYING. I THINK HE NEEDS HIS BOTTLE.

Alzheimer's or dementia walk right out the front door and wander off, sometimes in broad daylight.

It's amazing how far they can get, how easily they're ignored by the people they pass on the street.

As if seeing an old woman walking down the street, wearing nothing but her bathrobe, is perfectly normal.

At least Dorothy here will finally get the peace she deserves.

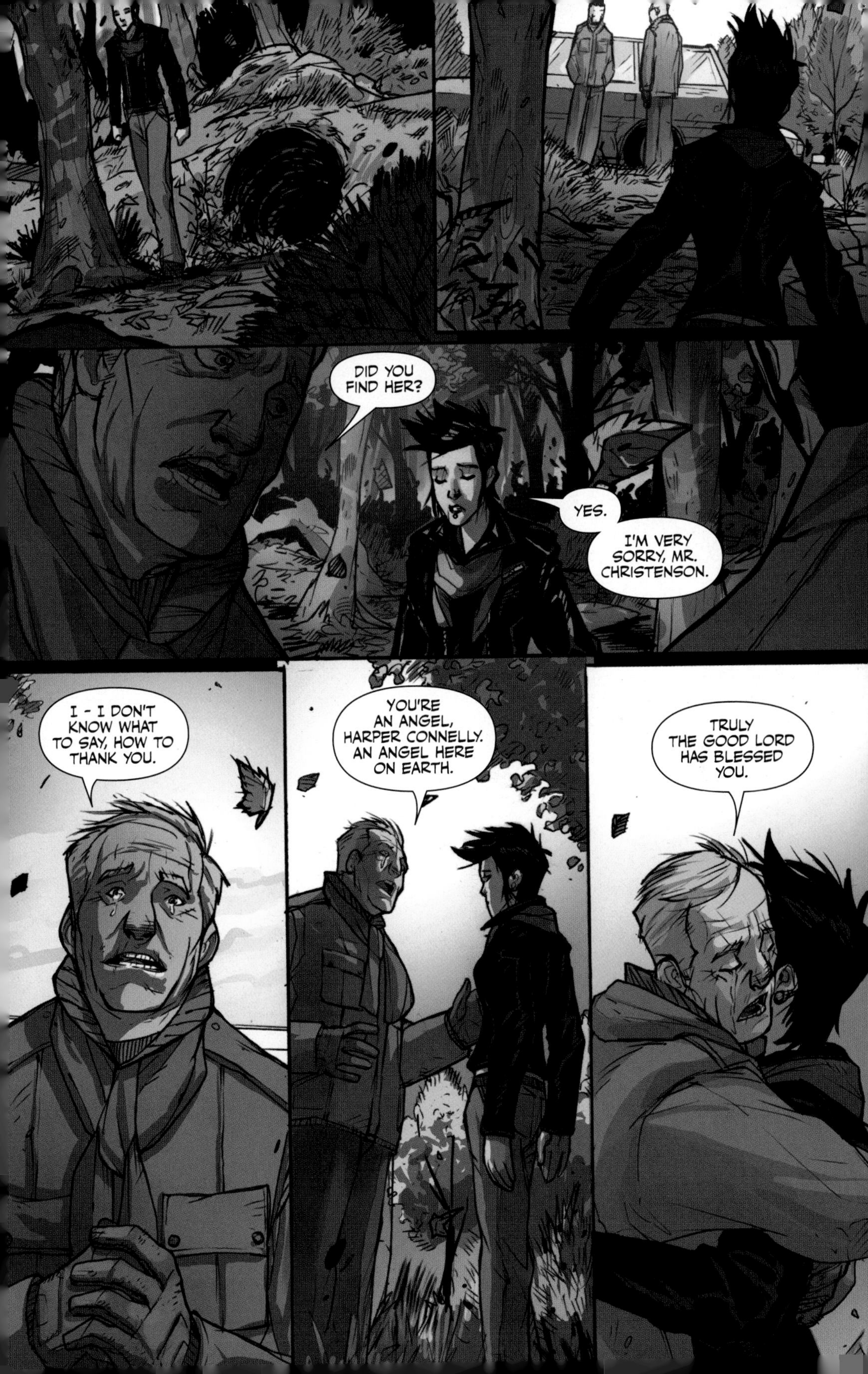
DID YOU FIND HER?
YES.
I'M VERY SORRY, MR. CHRISTENSON.
I - I DON'T KNOW WHAT TO SAY, HOW TO THANK YOU.
YOU'RE AN ANGEL, HARPER CONNELLY. AN ANGEL HERE ON EARTH.
TRULY THE GOOD LORD HAS BLESSED YOU.

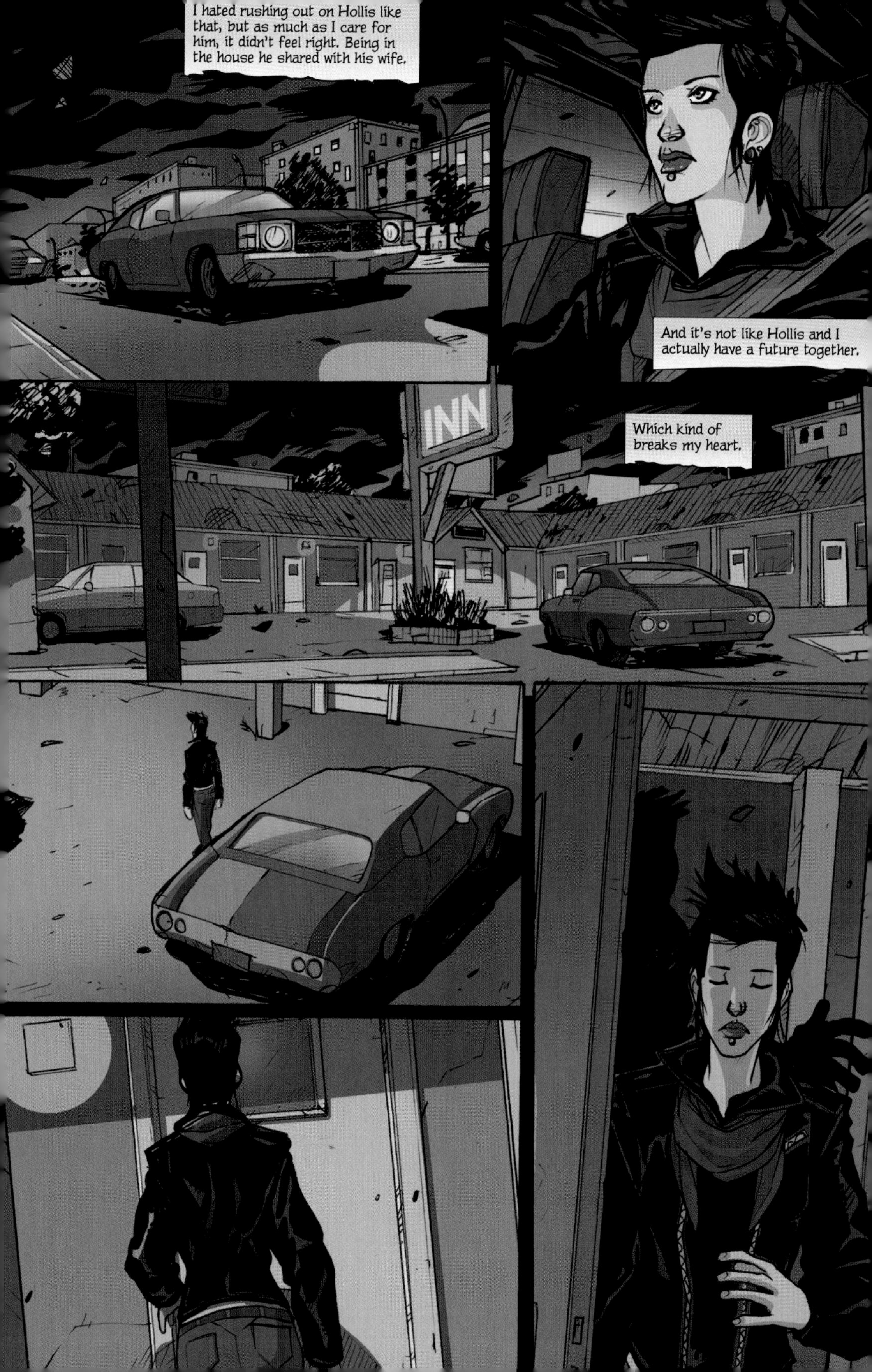
I hated rushing out on Hollis like that, but as much as I care for him, it didn't feel right. Being in the house he shared with his wife.
And it's not like Hollis and I actually have a future together.
INN
Which kind of breaks my heart.

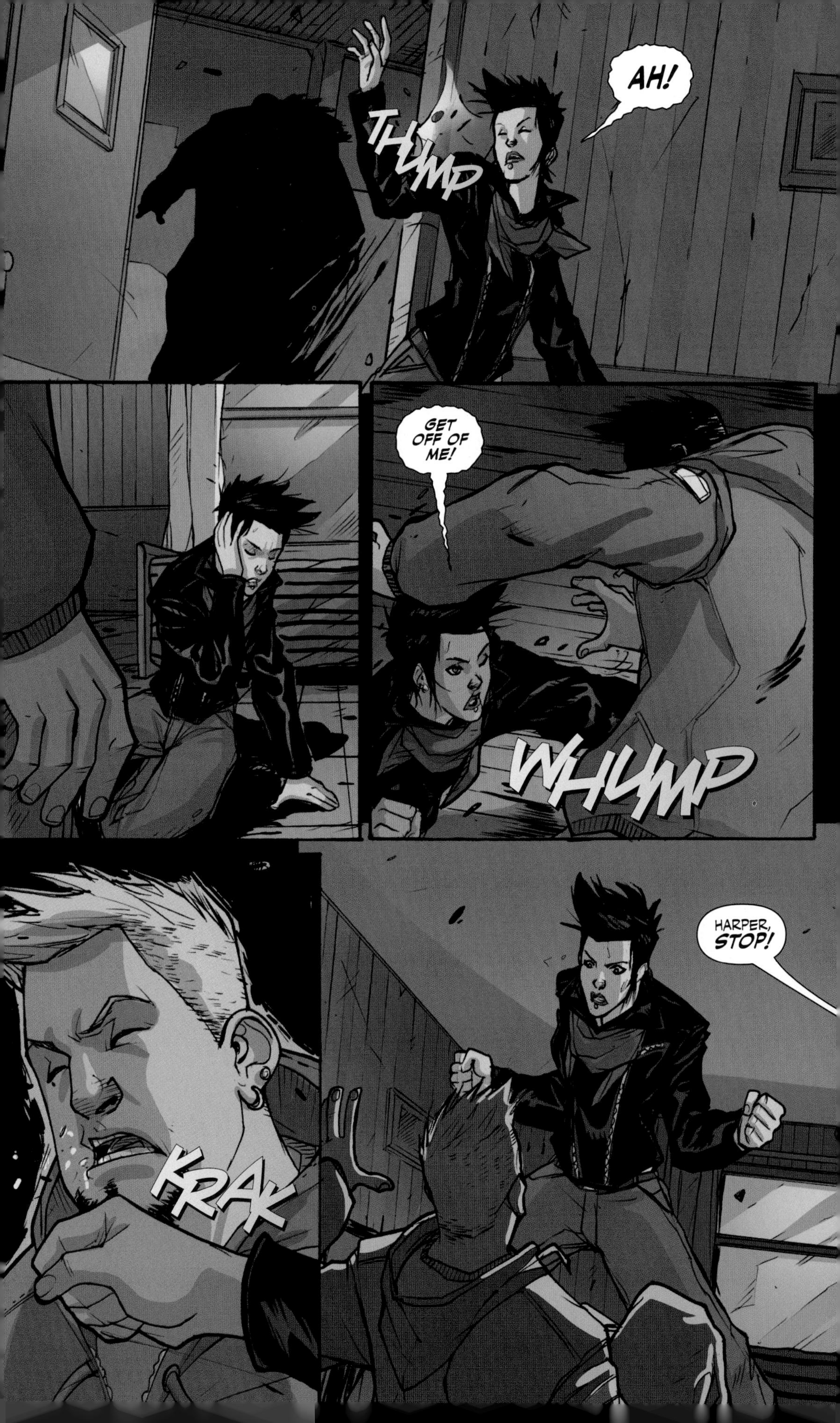
THUMP
AH!
GET OFF OF ME!
WHUMP
KRAK
HARPER, STOP!

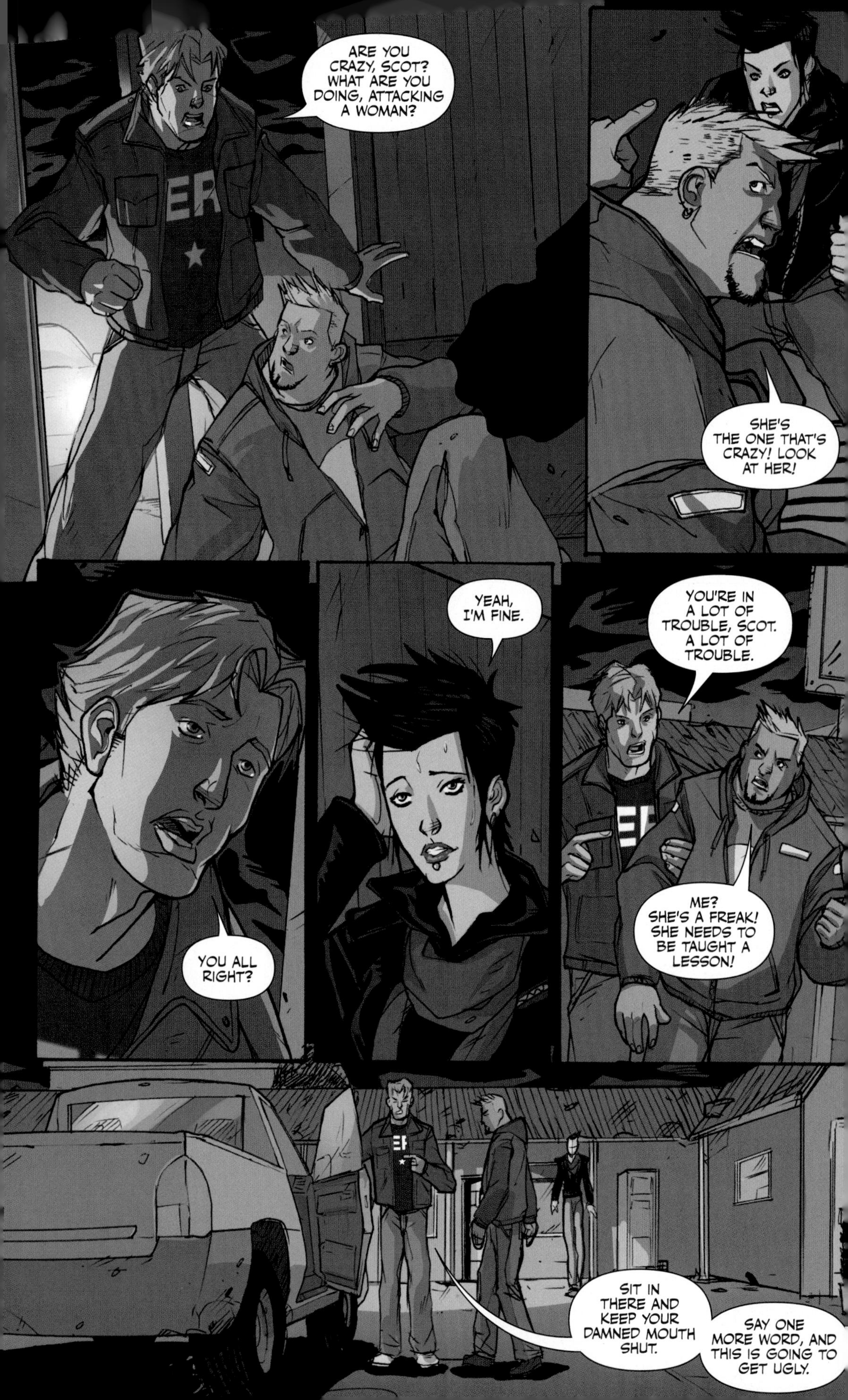
ARE YOU CRAZY, SCOT? WHAT ARE YOU DOING, ATTACKING A WOMAN?
SHE'S THE ONE THAT'S CRAZY! LOOK AT HER!
YOU ALL RIGHT?
YEAH, I'M FINE.
YOU'RE IN A LOT OF TROUBLE, SCOT. A LOT OF TROUBLE.
ME? SHE'S A FREAK! SHE NEEDS TO BE TAUGHT A LESSON!
SIT IN THERE AND KEEP YOUR DAMNED MOUTH SHUT.
SAY ONE MORE WORD, AND THIS IS GOING TO GET UGLY.

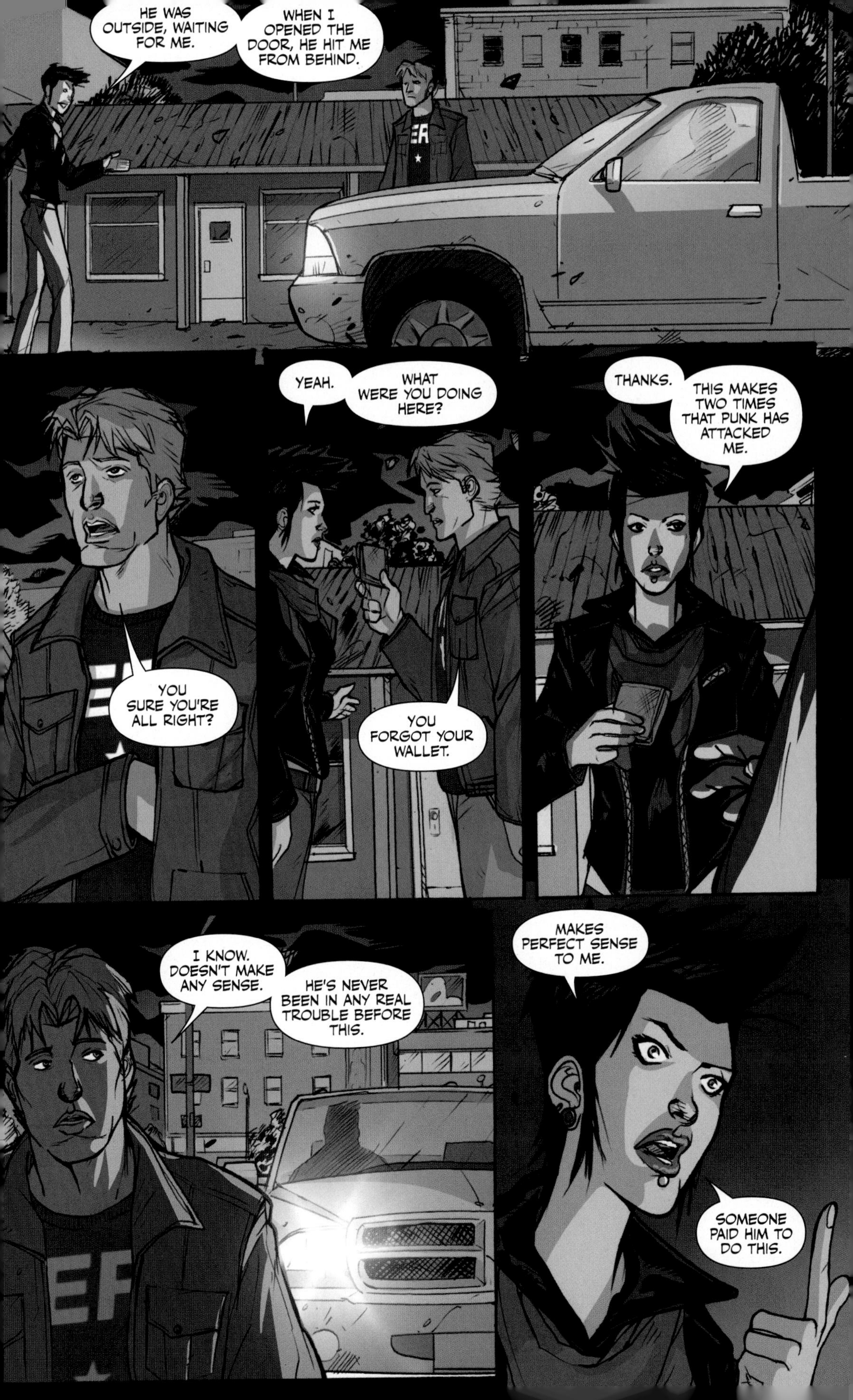
HE WAS OUTSIDE, WAITING FOR ME.
WHEN I OPENED THE DOOR, HE HIT ME FROM BEHIND.
YOU SURE YOU'RE ALL RIGHT?
YEAH.
WHAT WERE YOU DOING HERE?
YOU FORGOT YOUR WALLET.
THANKS.
THIS MAKES TWO TIMES THAT PUNK HAS ATTACKED ME.
I KNOW. DOESN'T MAKE ANY SENSE.
HE'S NEVER BEEN IN ANY REAL TROUBLE BEFORE THIS.
MAKES PERFECT SENSE TO ME.
SOMEONE PAID HIM TO DO THIS.

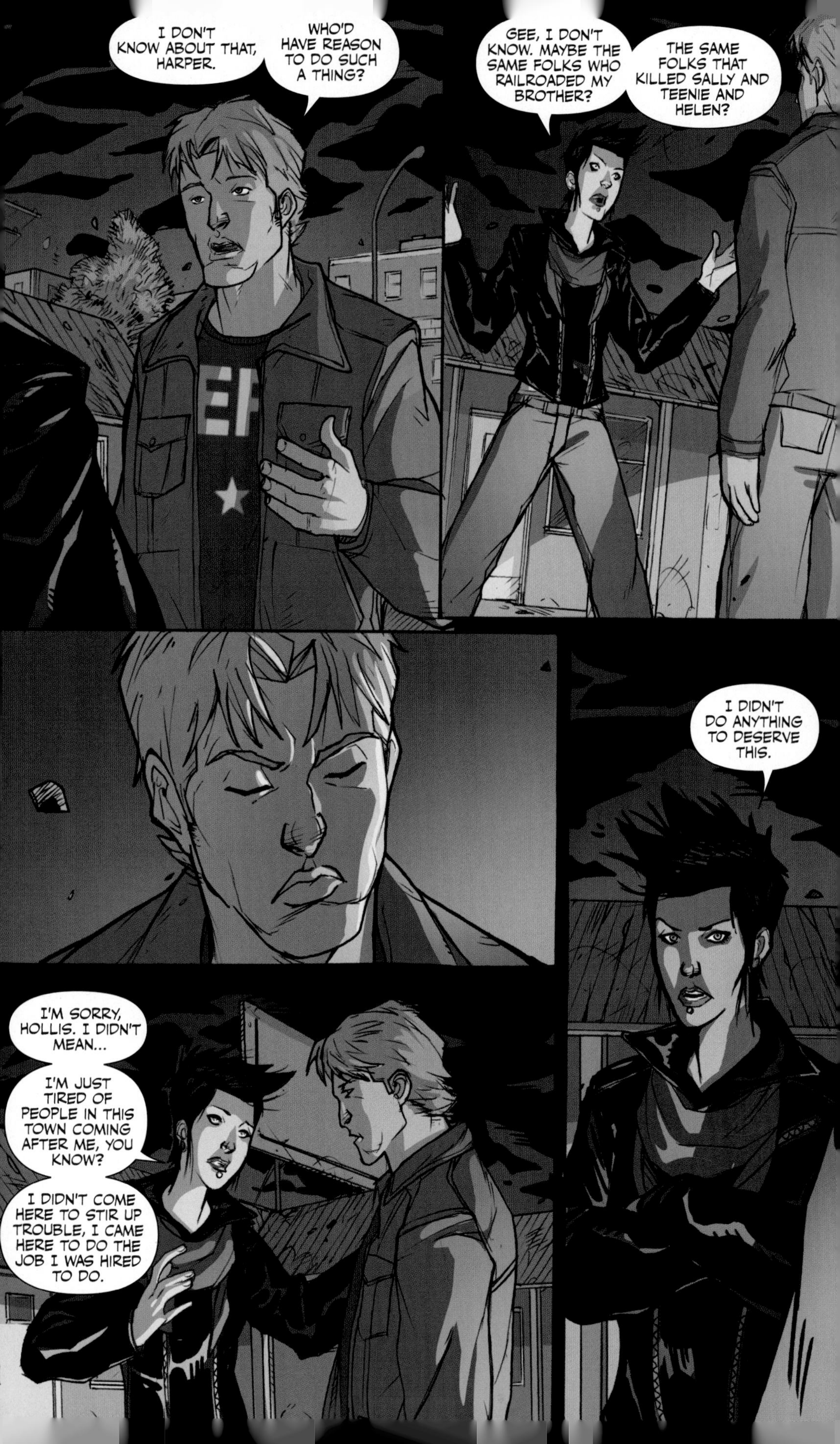
I DON'T KNOW ABOUT THAT, HARPER.
WHO'D HAVE REASON TO DO SUCH A THING?
GEE, I DON'T KNOW. MAYBE THE SAME FOLKS WHO RAILROADED MY BROTHER?
THE SAME FOLKS THAT KILLED SALLY AND TEENIE AND HELEN?
I DIDN'T DO ANYTHING TO DESERVE THIS.
I'M SORRY, HOLLIS. I DIDN'T MEAN...
I'M JUST TIRED OF PEOPLE IN THIS TOWN COMING AFTER ME, YOU KNOW?
I DIDN'T COME HERE TO STIR UP TROUBLE, I CAME HERE TO DO THE JOB I WAS HIRED TO DO.

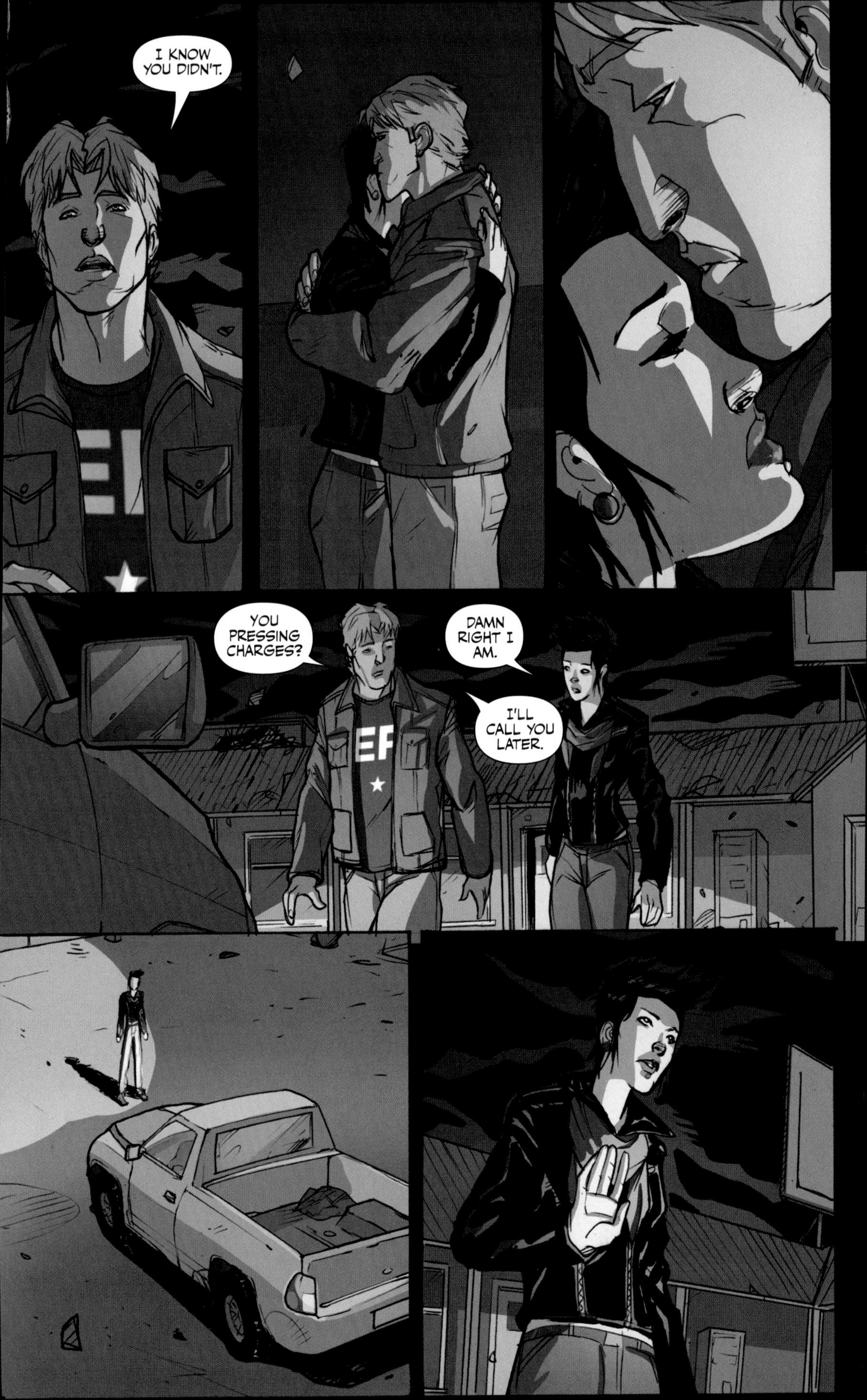
I KNOW YOU DIDN'T.
YOU PRESSING CHARGES?
DAMN RIGHT I AM.
I'LL CALL YOU LATER.

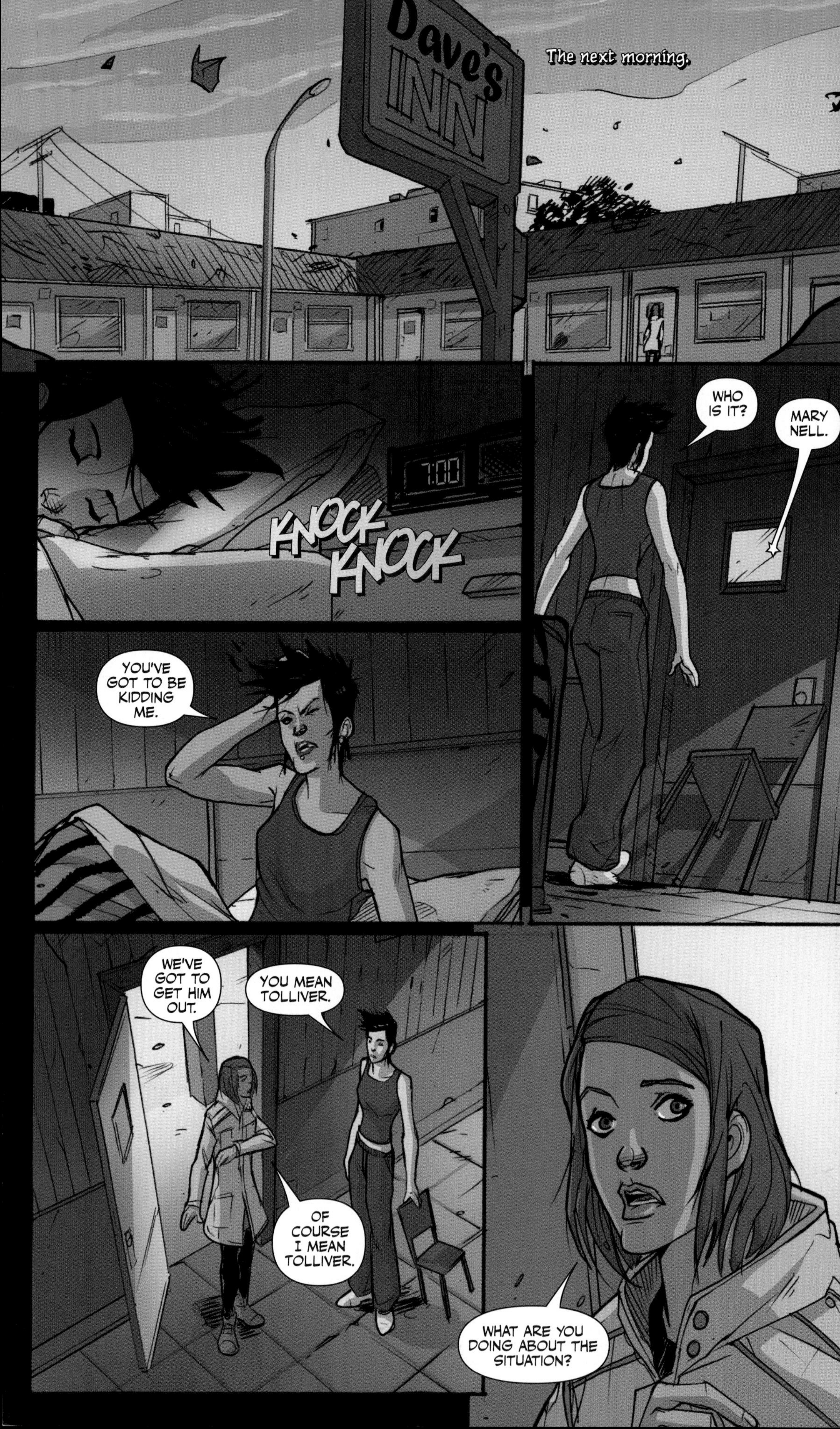

Dave's INN
The next morning.
7:00
KNOCK KNOCK
WHO IS IT?
MARY NELL.
YOU'VE GOT TO BE KIDDING ME.
WE'VE GOT TO GET HIM OUT.
YOU MEAN TOLLIVER.
OF COURSE I MEAN TOLLIVER.
WHAT ARE YOU DOING ABOUT THE SITUATION?

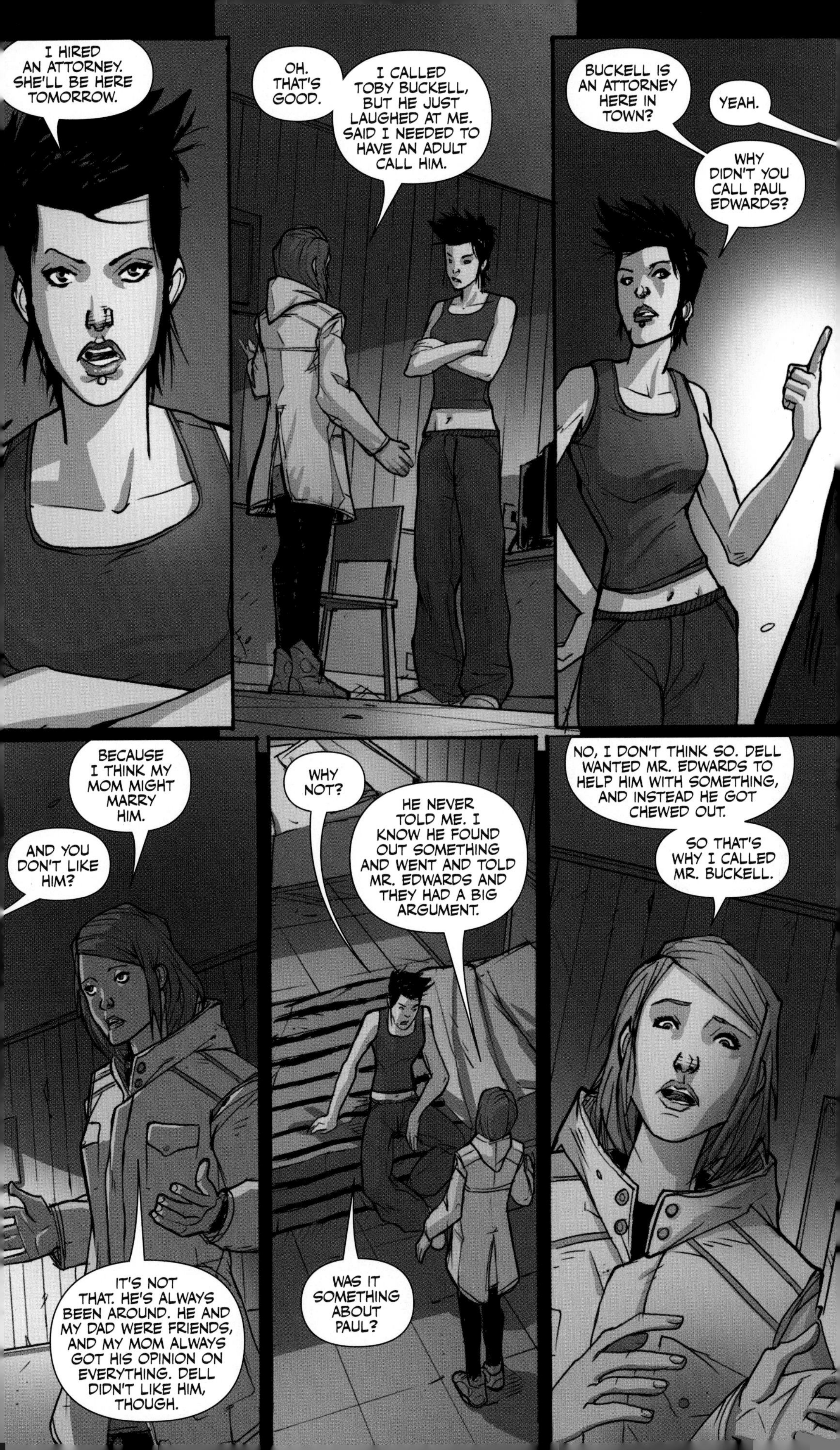

I HIRED AN ATTORNEY. SHE'LL BE HERE TOMORROW.
OH. THAT'S GOOD.
I CALLED TOBY BUCKELL, BUT HE JUST LAUGHED AT ME. SAID I NEEDED TO HAVE AN ADULT CALL HIM.
BUCKELL IS AN ATTORNEY HERE IN TOWN?
YEAH.
WHY DIDN'T YOU CALL PAUL EDWARDS?
BECAUSE I THINK MY MOM MIGHT MARRY HIM.
AND YOU DON'T LIKE HIM?
IT'S NOT THAT. HE'S ALWAYS BEEN AROUND. HE AND MY DAD WERE FRIENDS, AND MY MOM ALWAYS GOT HIS OPINION ON EVERYTHING. DELL DIDN'T LIKE HIM, THOUGH.
WHY NOT?
HE NEVER TOLD ME. I KNOW HE FOUND OUT SOMETHING AND WENT AND TOLD MR. EDWARDS AND THEY HAD A BIG ARGUMENT.
WAS IT SOMETHING ABOUT PAUL?
NO, I DON'T THINK SO. DELL WANTED MR. EDWARDS TO HELP HIM WITH SOMETHING, AND INSTEAD HE GOT CHEWED OUT.
SO THAT'S WHY I CALLED MR. BUCKELL.

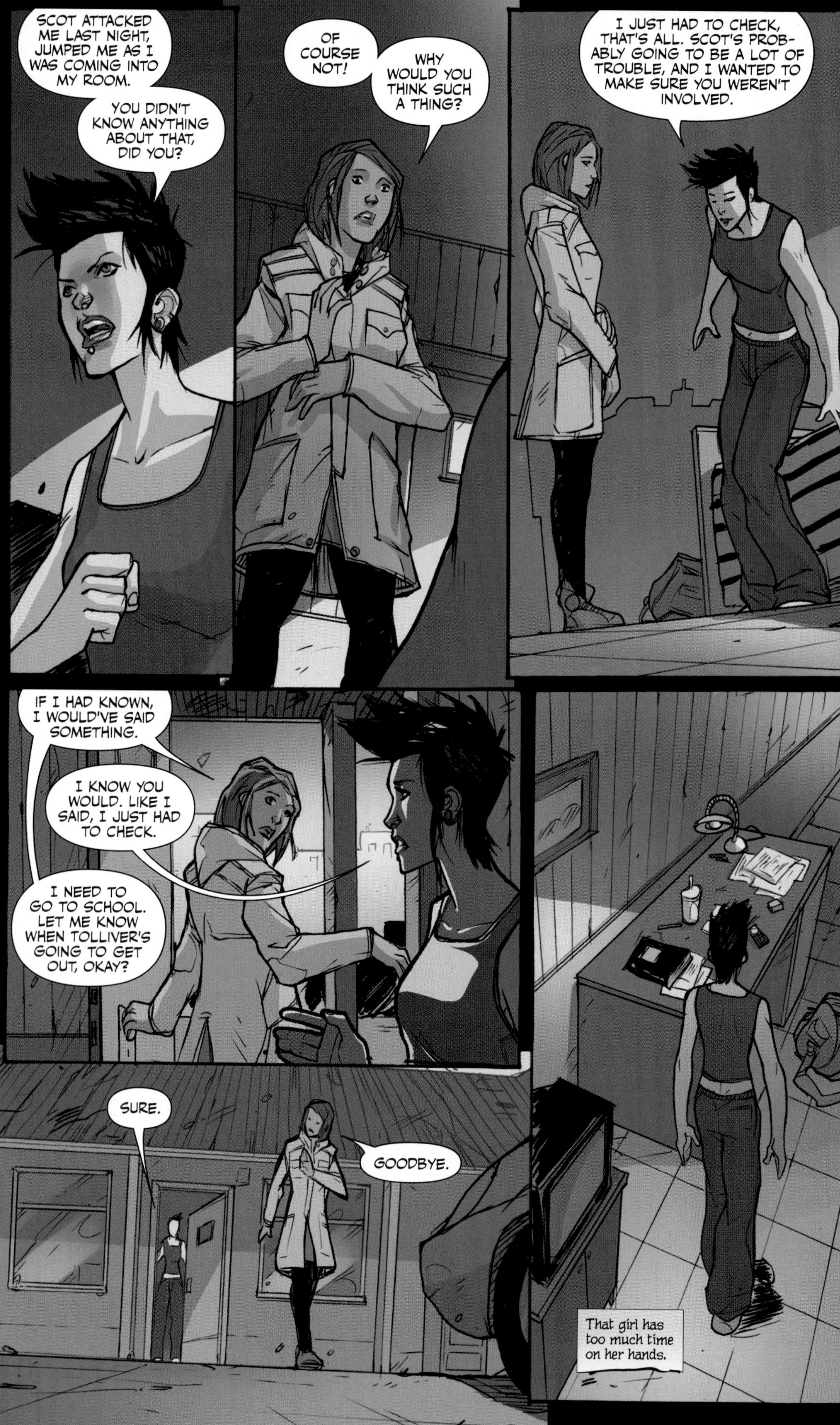
SCOT ATTACKED ME LAST NIGHT, JUMPED ME AS I WAS COMING INTO MY ROOM.
YOU DIDN'T KNOW ANYTHING ABOUT THAT, DID YOU?
OF COURSE NOT!
WHY WOULD YOU THINK SUCH A THING?
I JUST HAD TO CHECK, THAT'S ALL. SCOT'S PROBABLY GOING TO BE A LOT OF TROUBLE, AND I WANTED TO MAKE SURE YOU WEREN'T INVOLVED.
IF I HAD KNOWN, I WOULD'VE SAID SOMETHING.
I KNOW YOU WOULD. LIKE I SAID, I JUST HAD TO CHECK.
I NEED TO GO TO SCHOOL. LET ME KNOW WHEN TOLLIVER'S GOING TO GET OUT, OKAY?
SURE.
GOODBYE.
That girl has too much time on her hands.

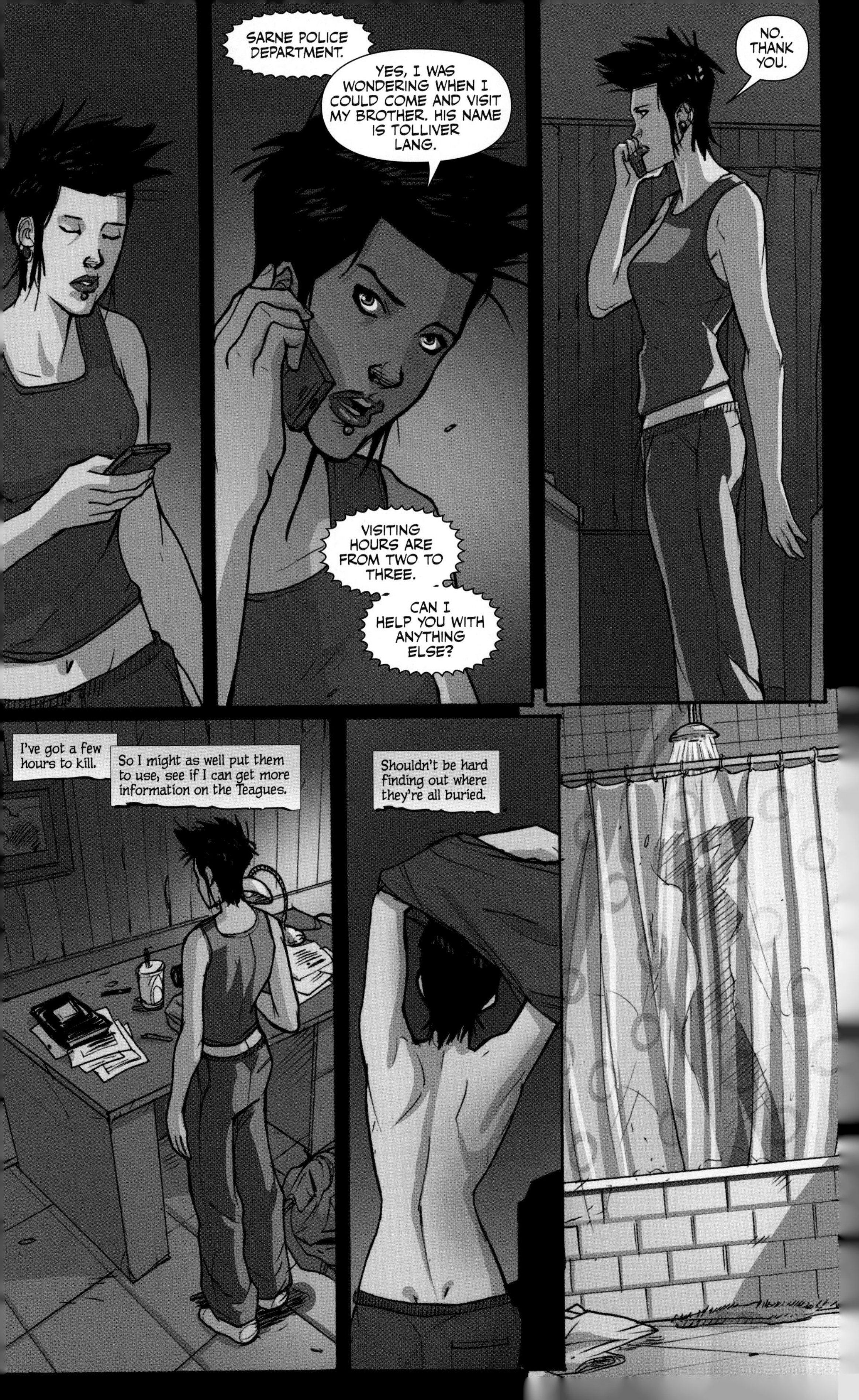
SARNE POLICE DEPARTMENT.
YES, I WAS WONDERING WHEN I COULD COME AND VISIT MY BROTHER. HIS NAME IS TOLLIVER LANG.
VISITING HOURS ARE FROM TWO TO THREE.
CAN I HELP YOU WITH ANYTHING ELSE?
NO. THANK YOU.
I've got a few hours to kill.
So I might as well put them to use, see if I can get more information on the Teagues.
Shouldn't be hard finding out where they're all buried.

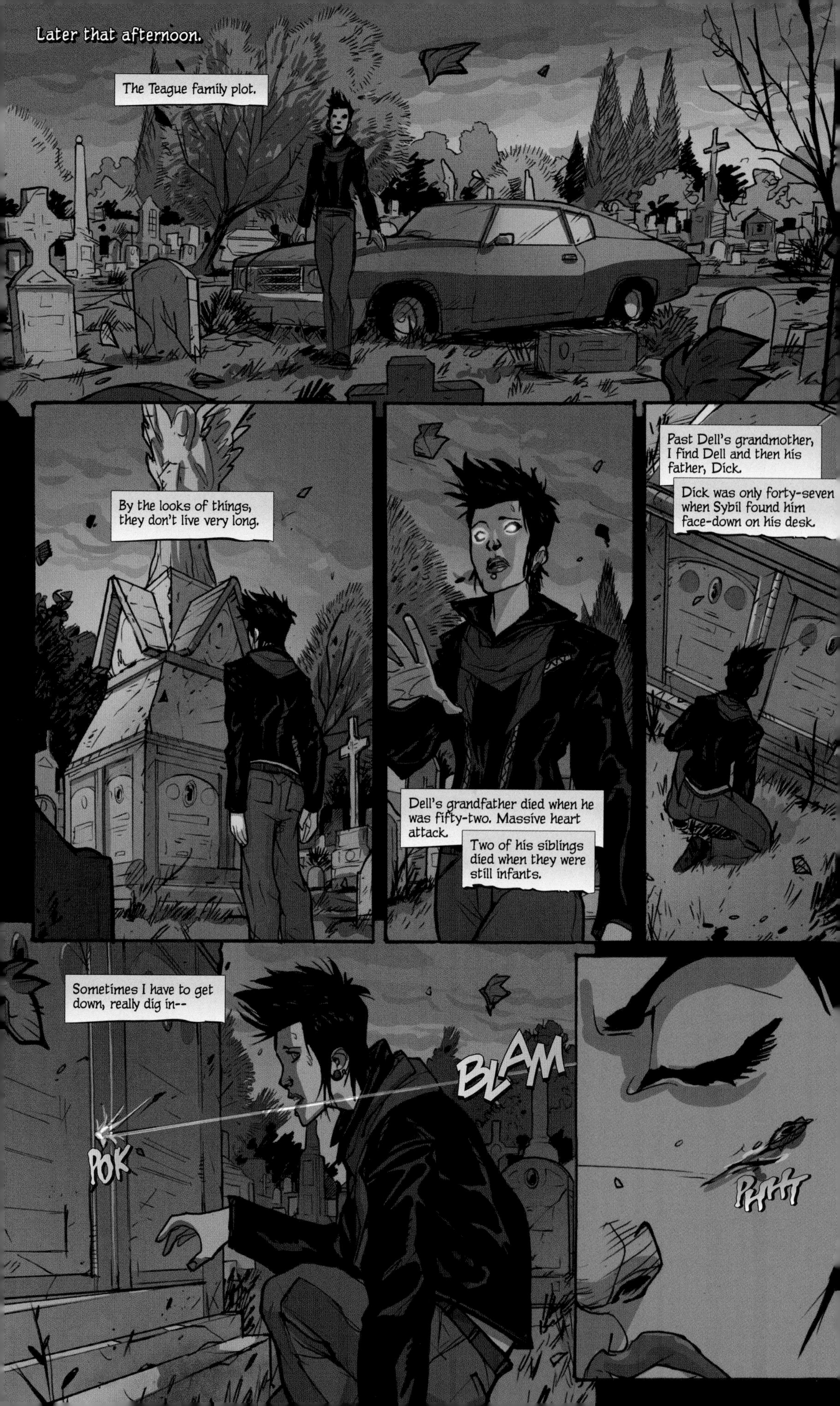

Later that afternoon.
The Teague family plot.
By the looks of things, they don't live very long.
Dell's grandfather died when he was fifty-two. Massive heart attack.
Two of his siblings died when they were still infants.
Past Dell's grandmother, I find Dell and then his father, Dick.
Dick was only forty-seven when Sybil found him face-down on his desk.
Sometimes I have to get down, really dig in--
BLAM
POK
PHHT

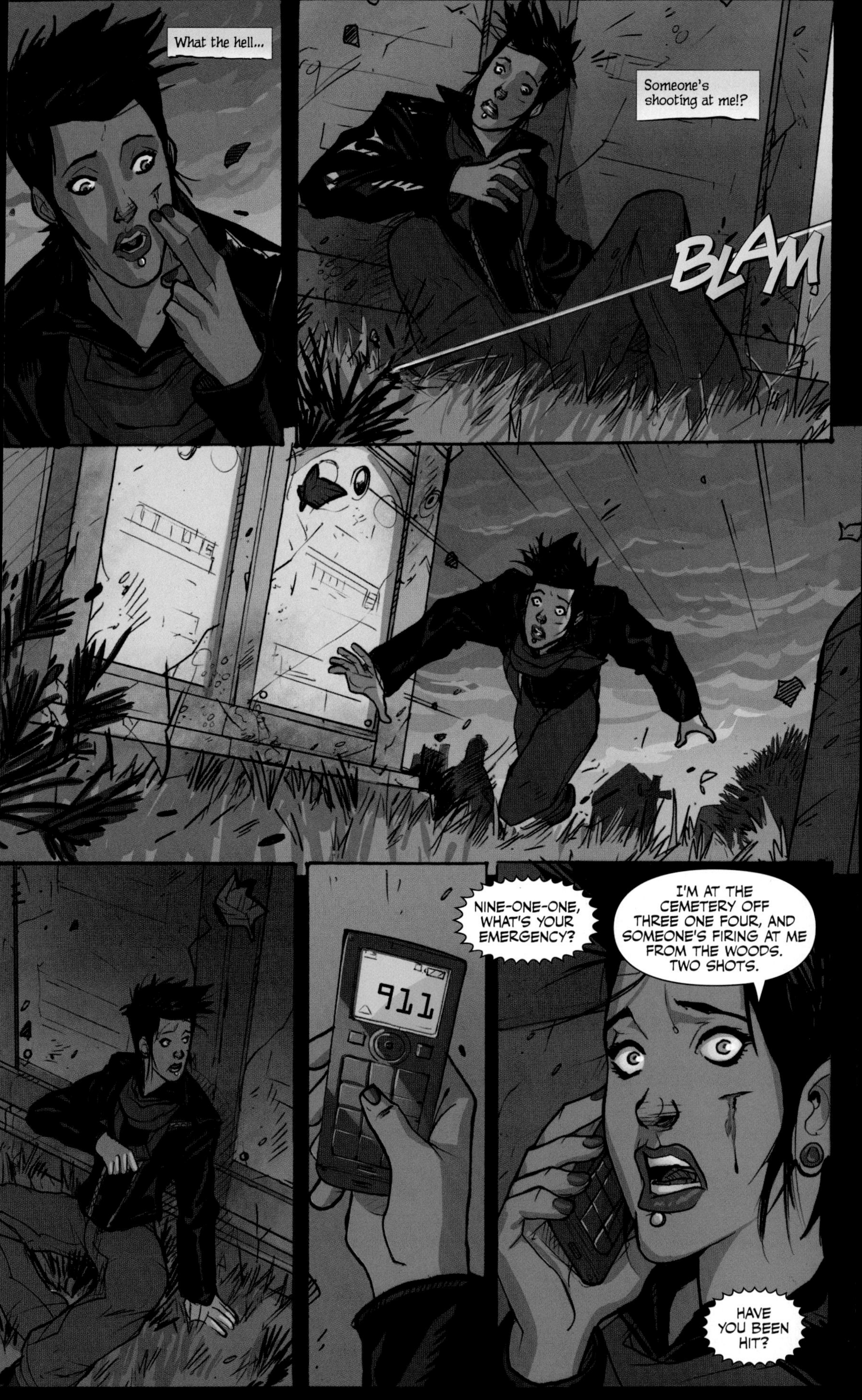
What the hell...
Someone's shooting at me!?
BLAM
911
NINE-ONE-ONE, WHAT'S YOUR EMERGENCY?
I'M AT THE CEMETERY OFF THREE ONE FOUR, AND SOMEONE'S FIRING AT ME FROM THE WOODS. TWO SHOTS.
HAVE YOU BEEN HIT?

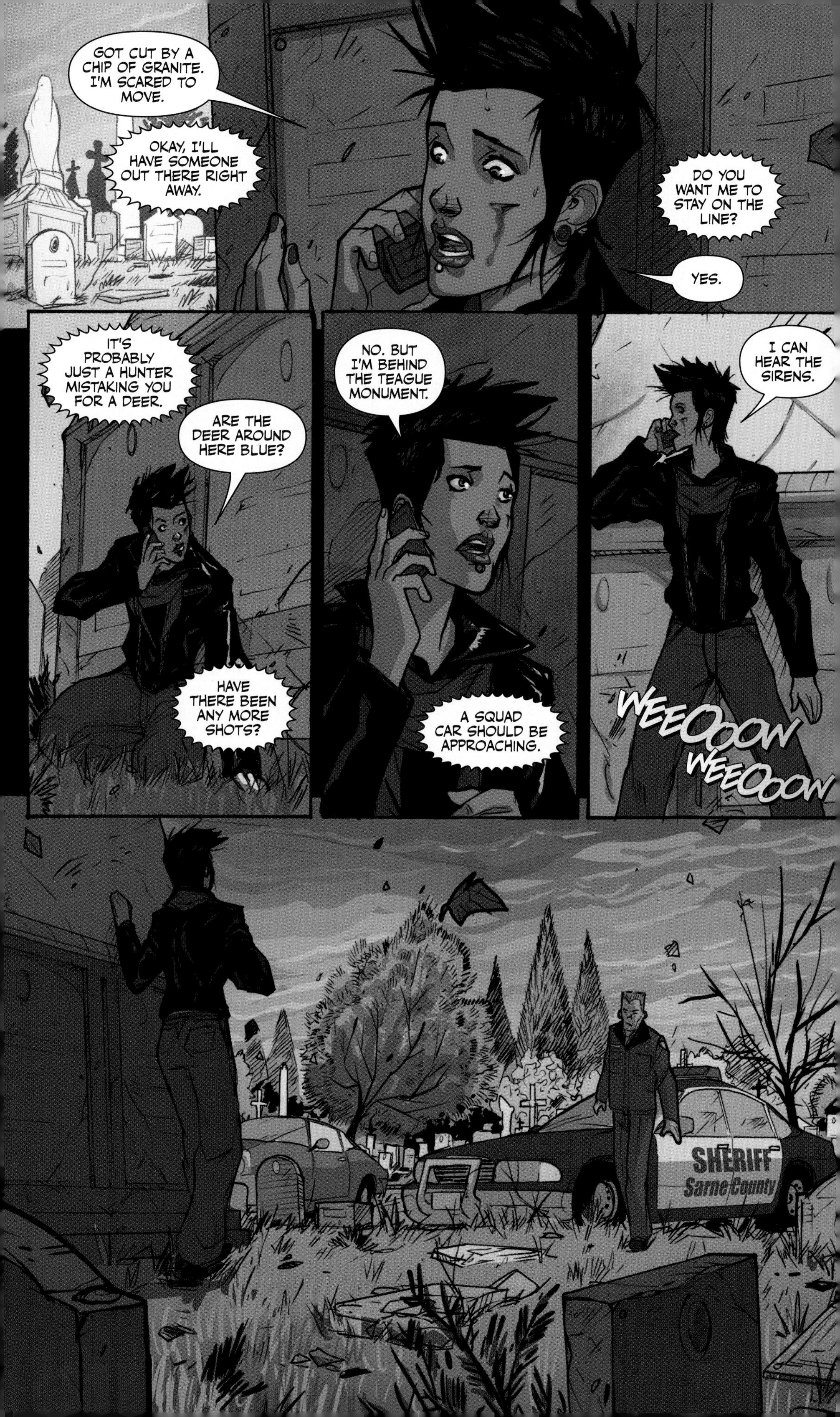
GOT CUT BY A CHIP OF GRANITE. I'M SCARED TO MOVE.
OKAY, I'LL HAVE SOMEONE OUT THERE RIGHT AWAY.
DO YOU WANT ME TO STAY ON THE LINE?
YES.
IT'S PROBABLY JUST A HUNTER MISTAKING YOU FOR A DEER.
ARE THE DEER AROUND HERE BLUE?
HAVE THERE BEEN ANY MORE SHOTS?
NO. BUT I'M BEHIND THE TEAGUE MONUMENT.
A SQUAD CAR SHOULD BE APPROACHING.
I CAN HEAR THE SIRENS.
WEEOOOOW
WEEOOOOW
SHERIFF
Sarne County

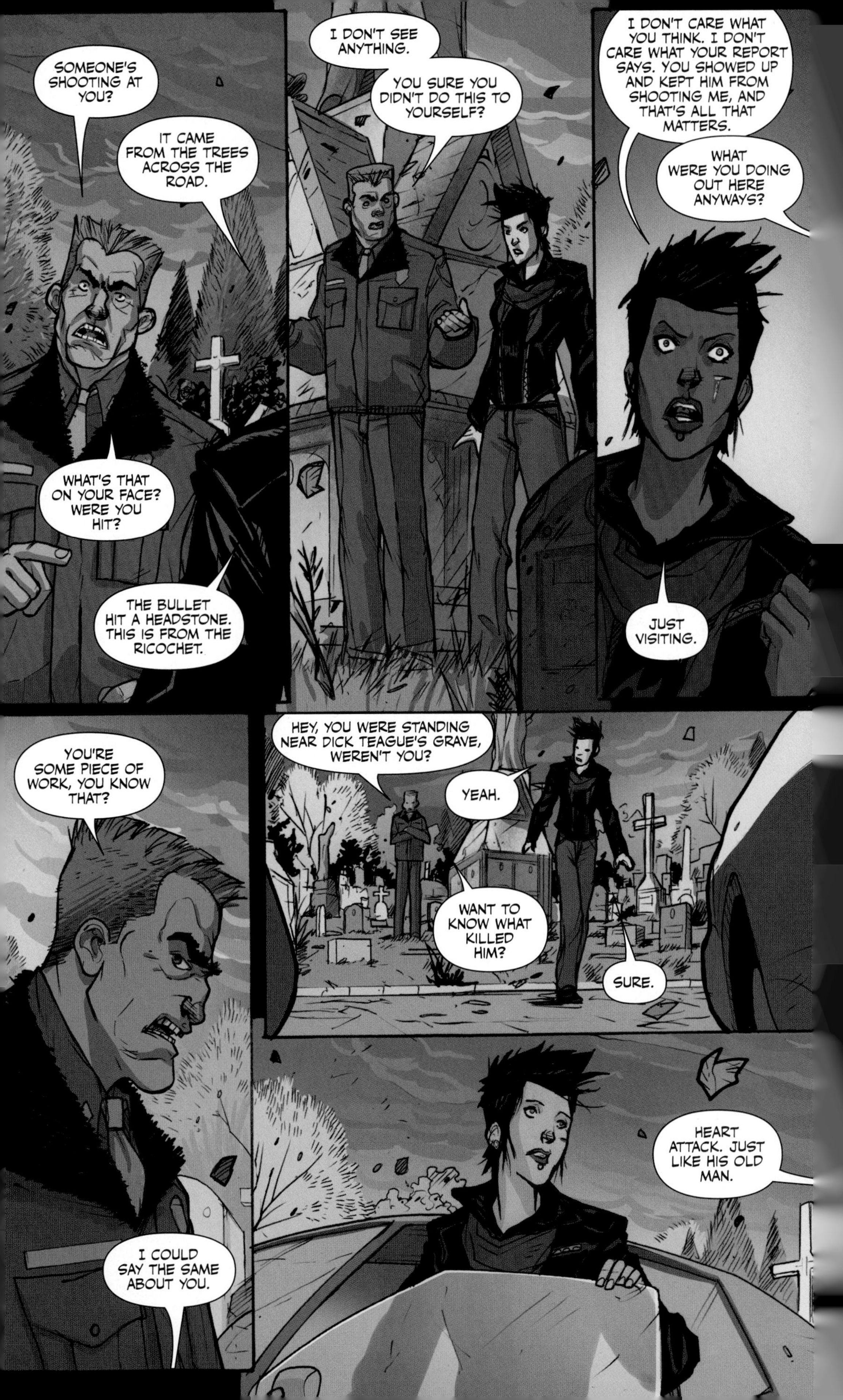
SOMEONE'S SHOOTING AT YOU?
IT CAME FROM THE TREES ACROSS THE ROAD.
WHAT'S THAT ON YOUR FACE? WERE YOU HIT?
THE BULLET HIT A HEADSTONE. THIS IS FROM THE RICOCHET.
I DON'T SEE ANYTHING.
YOU SURE YOU DIDN'T DO THIS TO YOURSELF?
I DON'T CARE WHAT YOU THINK. I DON'T CARE WHAT YOUR REPORT SAYS. YOU SHOWED UP AND KEPT HIM FROM SHOOTING ME, AND THAT'S ALL THAT MATTERS.
WHAT WERE YOU DOING OUT HERE ANYWAYS?
JUST VISITING.
YOU'RE SOME PIECE OF WORK, YOU KNOW THAT?
I COULD SAY THE SAME ABOUT YOU.
HEY, YOU WERE STANDING NEAR DICK TEAGUE'S GRAVE, WEREN'T YOU?
YEAH.
WANT TO KNOW WHAT KILLED HIM?
SURE.
HEART ATTACK. JUST LIKE HIS OLD MAN.

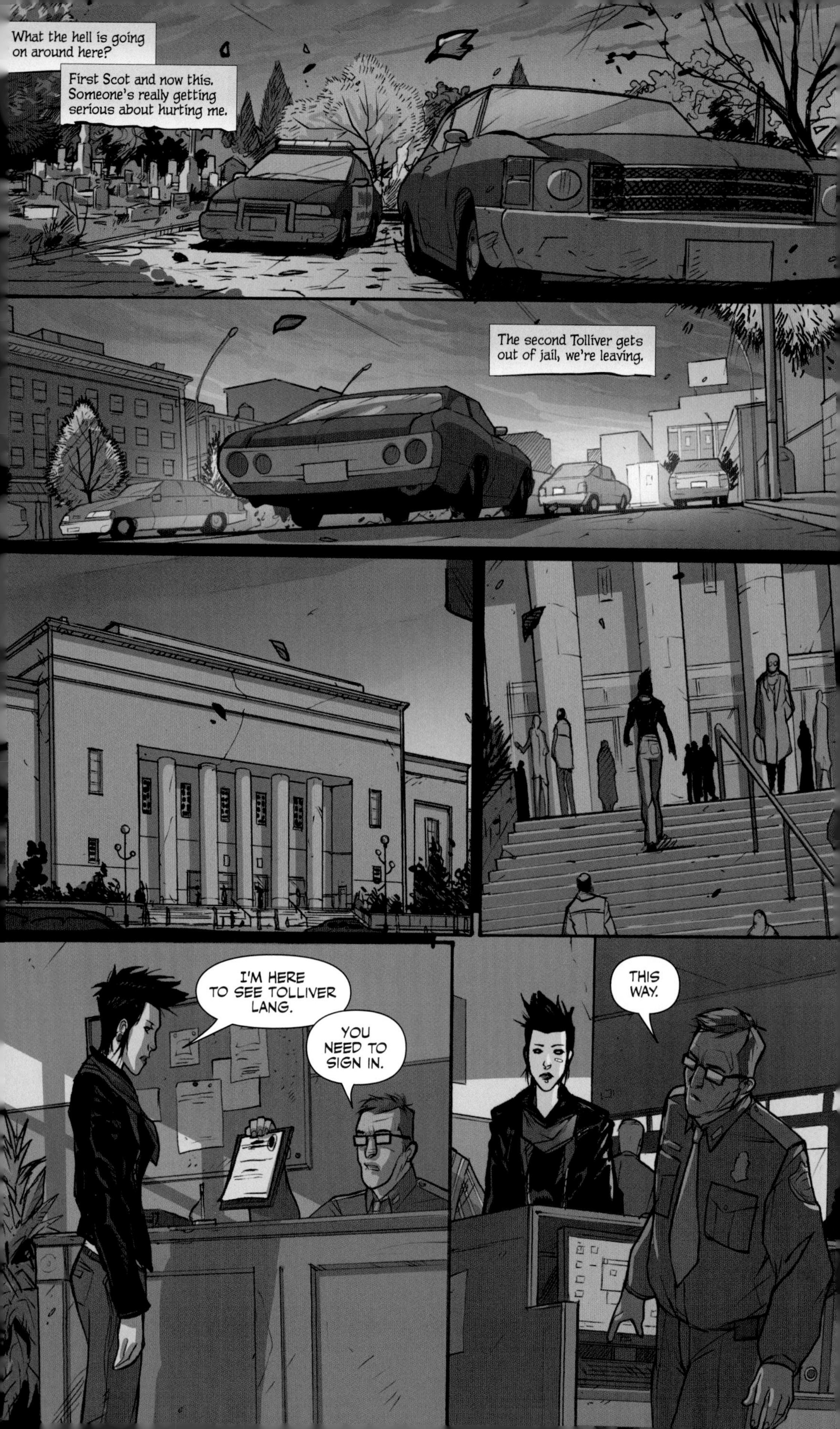
What the hell is going on around here?
First Scot and now this. Someone's really getting serious about hurting me.
The second Tolliver gets out of jail, we're leaving.
I'M HERE TO SEE TOLLIVER LANG.
YOU NEED TO SIGN IN.
THIS WAY.

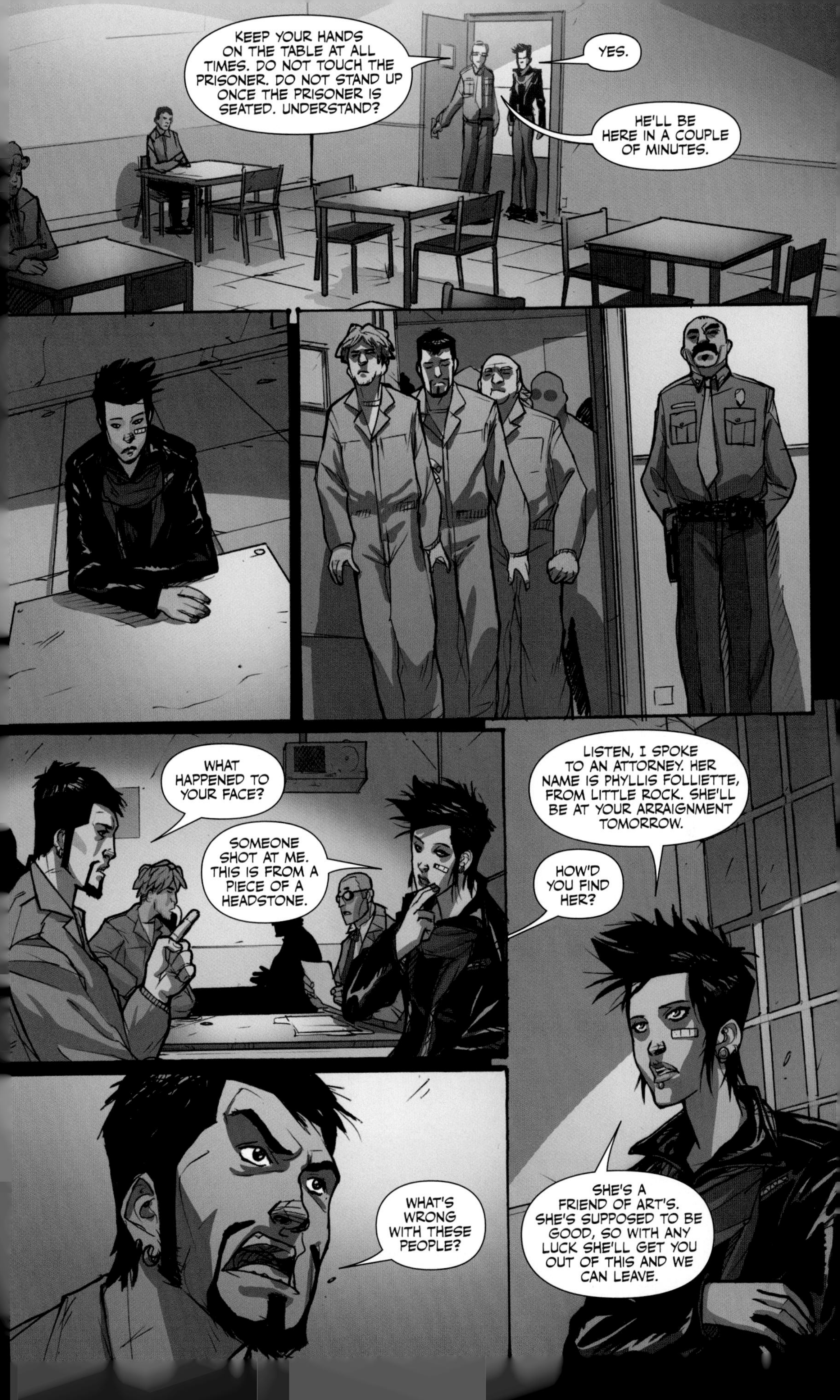
KEEP YOUR HANDS ON THE TABLE AT ALL TIMES. DO NOT TOUCH THE PRISONER. DO NOT STAND UP ONCE THE PRISONER IS SEATED. UNDERSTAND?
YES.
HE'LL BE HERE IN A COUPLE OF MINUTES.
WHAT HAPPENED TO YOUR FACE?
SOMEONE SHOT AT ME. THIS IS FROM A PIECE OF A HEADSTONE.
LISTEN, I SPOKE TO AN ATTORNEY. HER NAME IS PHYLLIS FOLLIETTE, FROM LITTLE ROCK. SHE'LL BE AT YOUR ARRAIGNMENT TOMORROW.
HOW'D YOU FIND HER?
WHAT'S WRONG WITH THESE PEOPLE?
SHE'S A FRIEND OF ART'S. SHE'S SUPPOSED TO BE GOOD, SO WITH ANY LUCK SHE'LL GET YOU OUT OF THIS AND WE CAN LEAVE.

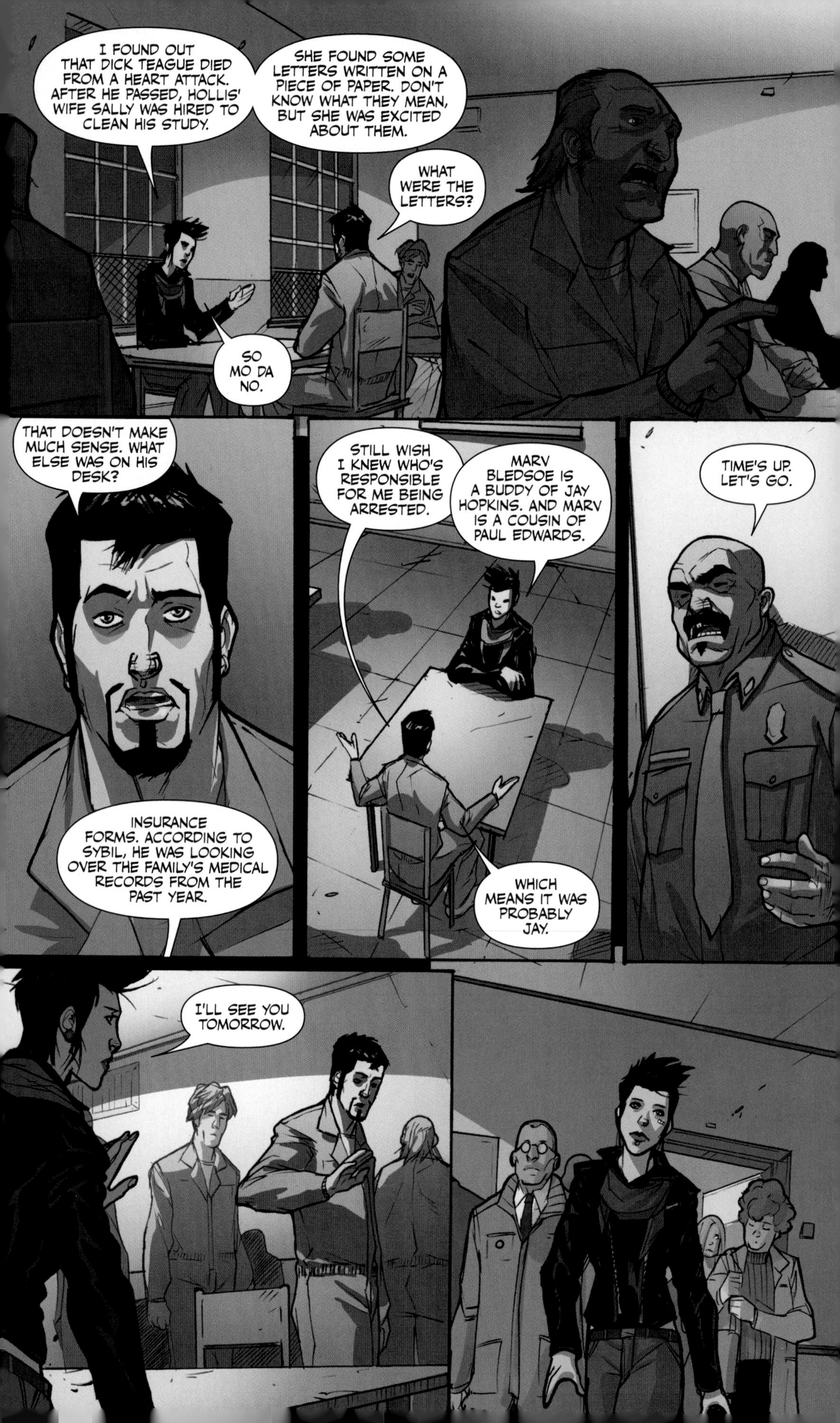

I FOUND OUT THAT DICK TEAGUE DIED FROM A HEART ATTACK. AFTER HE PASSED, HOLLIS' WIFE SALLY WAS HIRED TO CLEAN HIS STUDY.
SHE FOUND SOME LETTERS WRITTEN ON A PIECE OF PAPER. DON'T KNOW WHAT THEY MEAN, BUT SHE WAS EXCITED ABOUT THEM.
WHAT WERE THE LETTERS?
SO MO DA NO.
THAT DOESN'T MAKE MUCH SENSE. WHAT ELSE WAS ON HIS DESK?
INSURANCE FORMS. ACCORDING TO SYBIL, HE WAS LOOKING OVER THE FAMILY'S MEDICAL RECORDS FROM THE PAST YEAR.
STILL WISH I KNEW WHO'S RESPONSIBLE FOR ME BEING ARRESTED.
MARV BLEDSOE IS A BUDDY OF JAY HOPKINS. AND MARV IS A COUSIN OF PAUL EDWARDS.
WHICH MEANS IT WAS PROBABLY JAY.
TIME'S UP. LET'S GO.
I'LL SEE YOU TOMORROW.

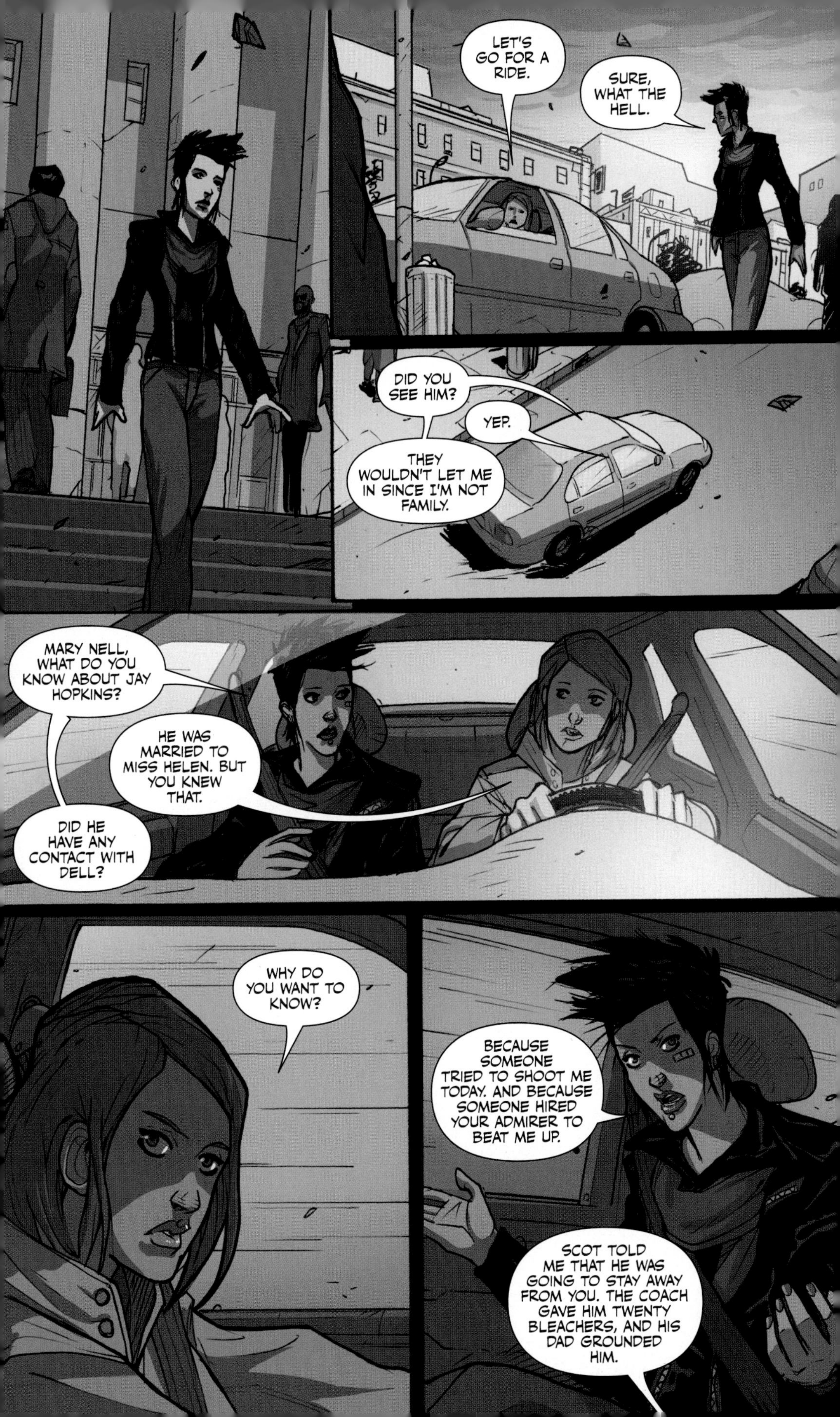
LET'S GO FOR A RIDE.
SURE, WHAT THE HELL.
DID YOU SEE HIM?
YEP.
THEY WOULDN'T LET ME IN SINCE I'M NOT FAMILY.
MARY NELL, WHAT DO YOU KNOW ABOUT JAY HOPKINS?
HE WAS MARRIED TO MISS HELEN. BUT YOU KNEW THAT.
DID HE HAVE ANY CONTACT WITH DELL?
WHY DO YOU WANT TO KNOW?
BECAUSE SOMEONE TRIED TO SHOOT ME TODAY. AND BECAUSE SOMEONE HIRED YOUR ADMIRER TO BEAT ME UP.
SCOT TOLD ME THAT HE WAS GOING TO STAY AWAY FROM YOU. THE COACH GAVE HIM TWENTY BLEACHERS, AND HIS DAD GROUNDED HIM.

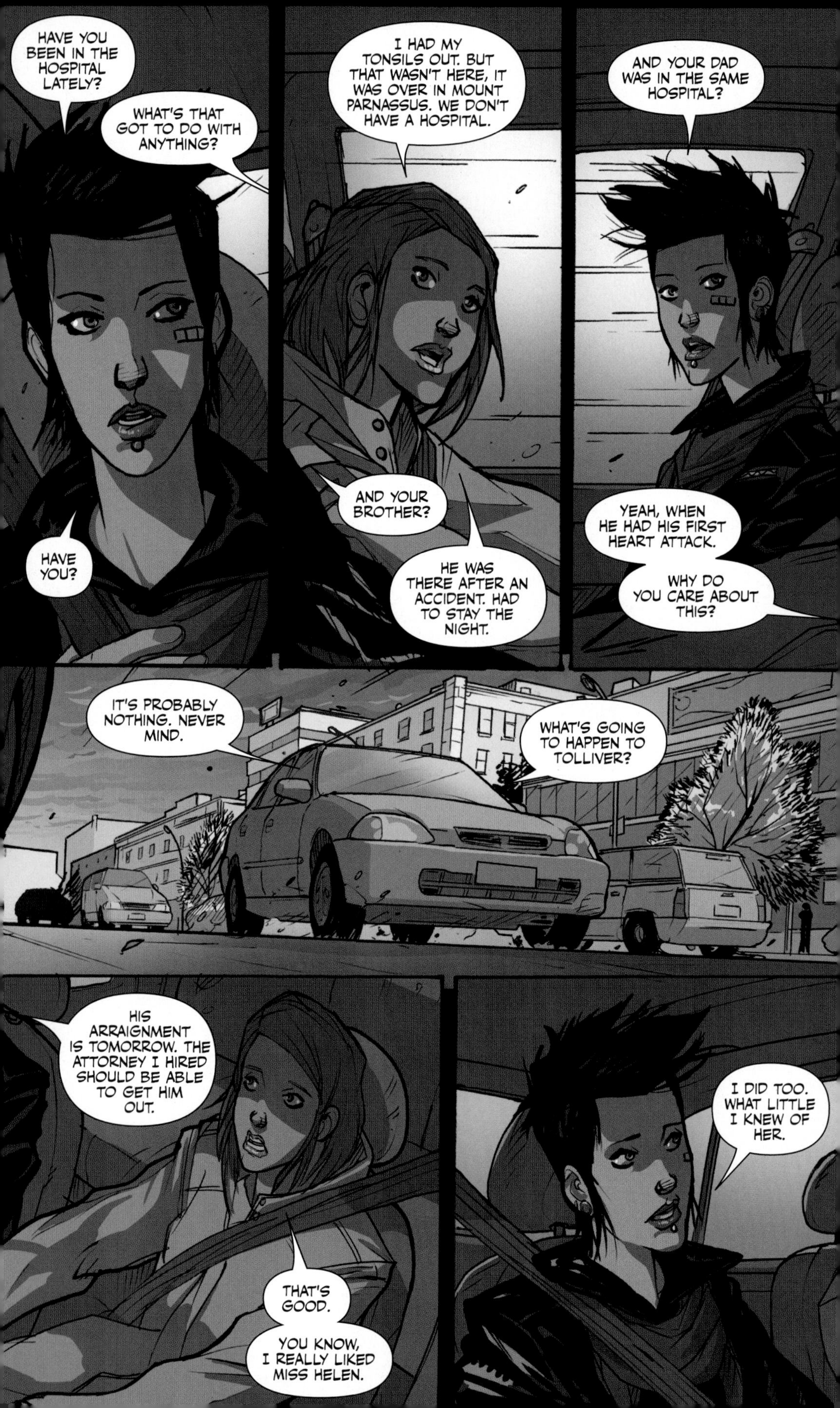
HAVE YOU BEEN IN THE HOSPITAL LATELY?
WHAT'S THAT GOT TO DO WITH ANYTHING?
HAVE YOU?
I HAD MY TONSILS OUT. BUT THAT WASN'T HERE, IT WAS OVER IN MOUNT PARNASSUS. WE DON'T HAVE A HOSPITAL.
AND YOUR BROTHER?
HE WAS THERE AFTER AN ACCIDENT. HAD TO STAY THE NIGHT.
AND YOUR DAD WAS IN THE SAME HOSPITAL?
YEAH, WHEN HE HAD HIS FIRST HEART ATTACK.
WHY DO YOU CARE ABOUT THIS?
IT'S PROBABLY NOTHING. NEVER MIND.
WHAT'S GOING TO HAPPEN TO TOLLIVER?
HIS ARRAIGNMENT IS TOMORROW. THE ATTORNEY I HIRED SHOULD BE ABLE TO GET HIM OUT.
THAT'S GOOD.
YOU KNOW, I REALLY LIKED MISS HELEN.
I DID TOO. WHAT LITTLE I KNEW OF HER.

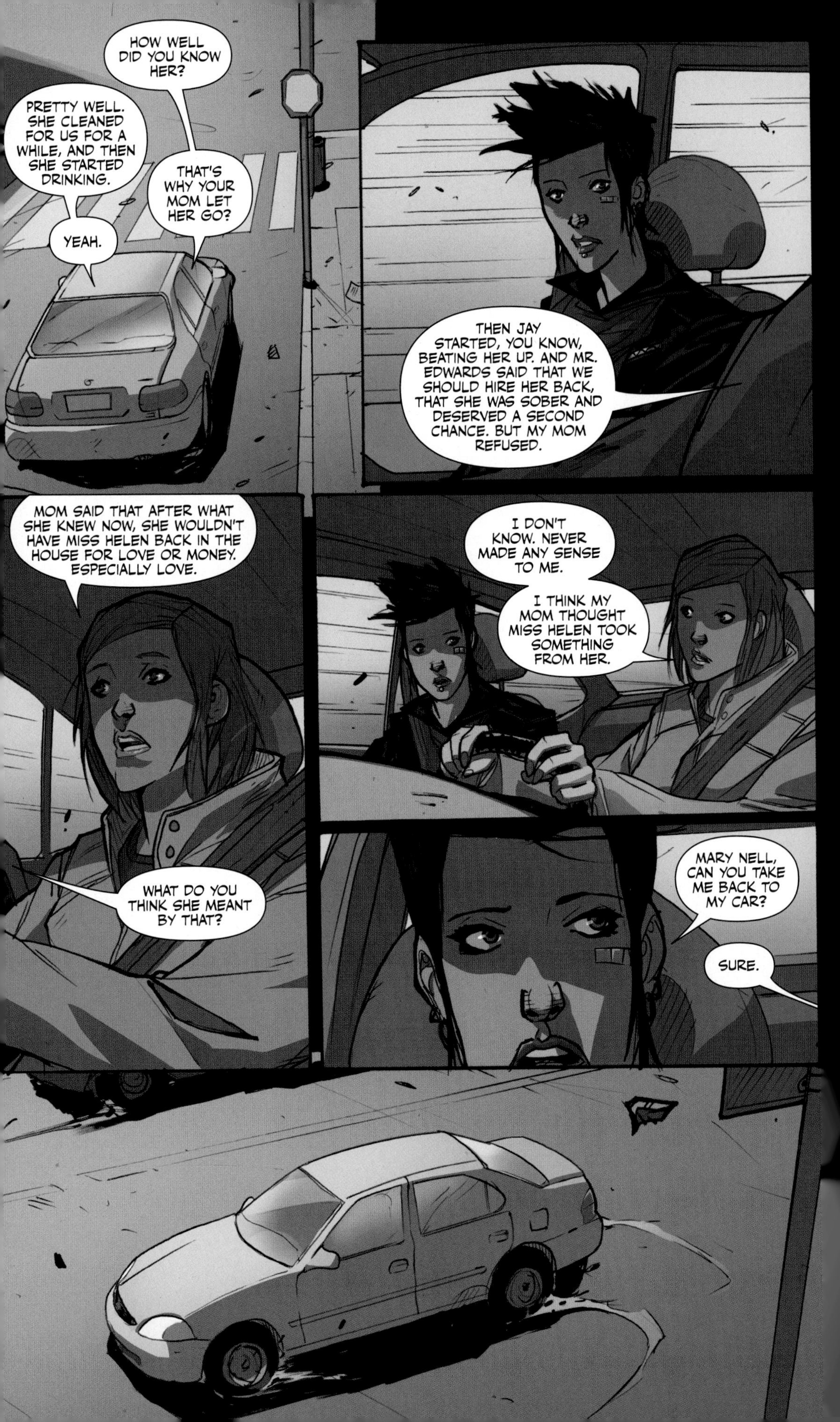
HOW WELL DID YOU KNOW HER?
PRETTY WELL. SHE CLEANED FOR US FOR A WHILE, AND THEN SHE STARTED DRINKING.
THAT'S WHY YOUR MOM LET HER GO?
YEAH.
THEN JAY STARTED, YOU KNOW, BEATING HER UP. AND MR. EDWARDS SAID THAT WE SHOULD HIRE HER BACK, THAT SHE WAS SOBER AND DESERVED A SECOND CHANCE. BUT MY MOM REFUSED.
MOM SAID THAT AFTER WHAT SHE KNEW NOW, SHE WOULDN'T HAVE MISS HELEN BACK IN THE HOUSE FOR LOVE OR MONEY. ESPECIALLY LOVE.
WHAT DO YOU THINK SHE MEANT BY THAT?
I DON'T KNOW. NEVER MADE ANY SENSE TO ME.
I THINK MY MOM THOUGHT MISS HELEN TOOK SOMETHING FROM HER.
MARY NELL, CAN YOU TAKE ME BACK TO MY CAR?
SURE.

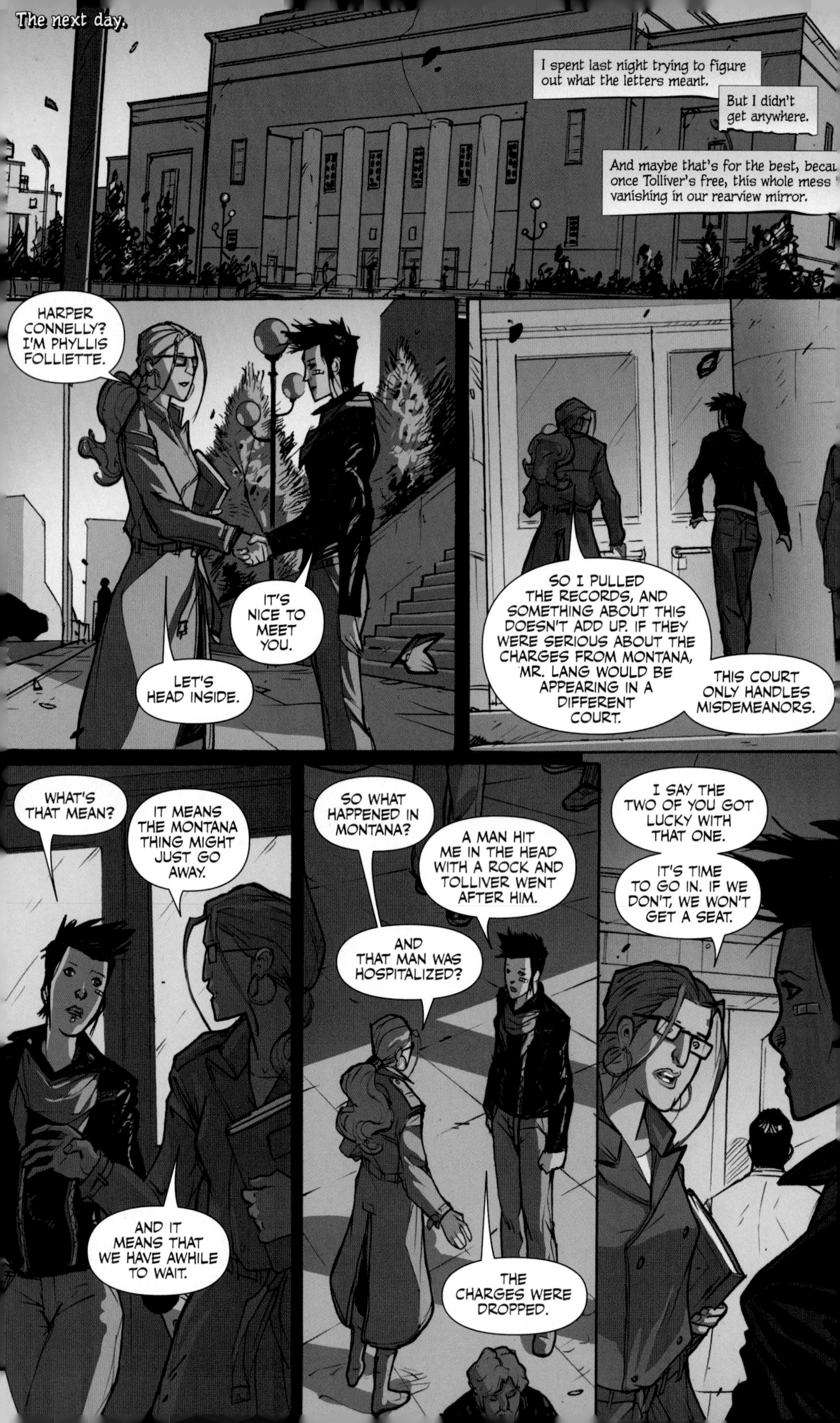
The next day.
I spent last night trying to figure out what the letters meant.
But I didn't get anywhere.
And maybe that's for the best, becau once Tolliver's free, this whole mess vanishing in our rearview mirror.
HARPER CONNELLY? I'M PHYLLIS FOLLIETTE.
IT'S NICE TO MEET YOU.
LET'S HEAD INSIDE.
SO I PULLED THE RECORDS, AND SOMETHING ABOUT THIS DOESN'T ADD UP. IF THEY WERE SERIOUS ABOUT THE CHARGES FROM MONTANA, MR. LANG WOULD BE APPEARING IN A DIFFERENT COURT.
THIS COURT ONLY HANDLES MISDEMEANORS.
WHAT'S THAT MEAN?
IT MEANS THE MONTANA THING MIGHT JUST GO AWAY.
AND IT MEANS THAT WE HAVE AWHILE TO WAIT.
SO WHAT HAPPENED IN MONTANA?
A MAN HIT ME IN THE HEAD WITH A ROCK AND TOLLIVER WENT AFTER HIM.
AND THAT MAN WAS HOSPITALIZED?
THE CHARGES WERE DROPPED.
I SAY THE TWO OF YOU GOT LUCKY WITH THAT ONE.
IT'S TIME TO GO IN. IF WE DON'T, WE WON'T GET A SEAT.

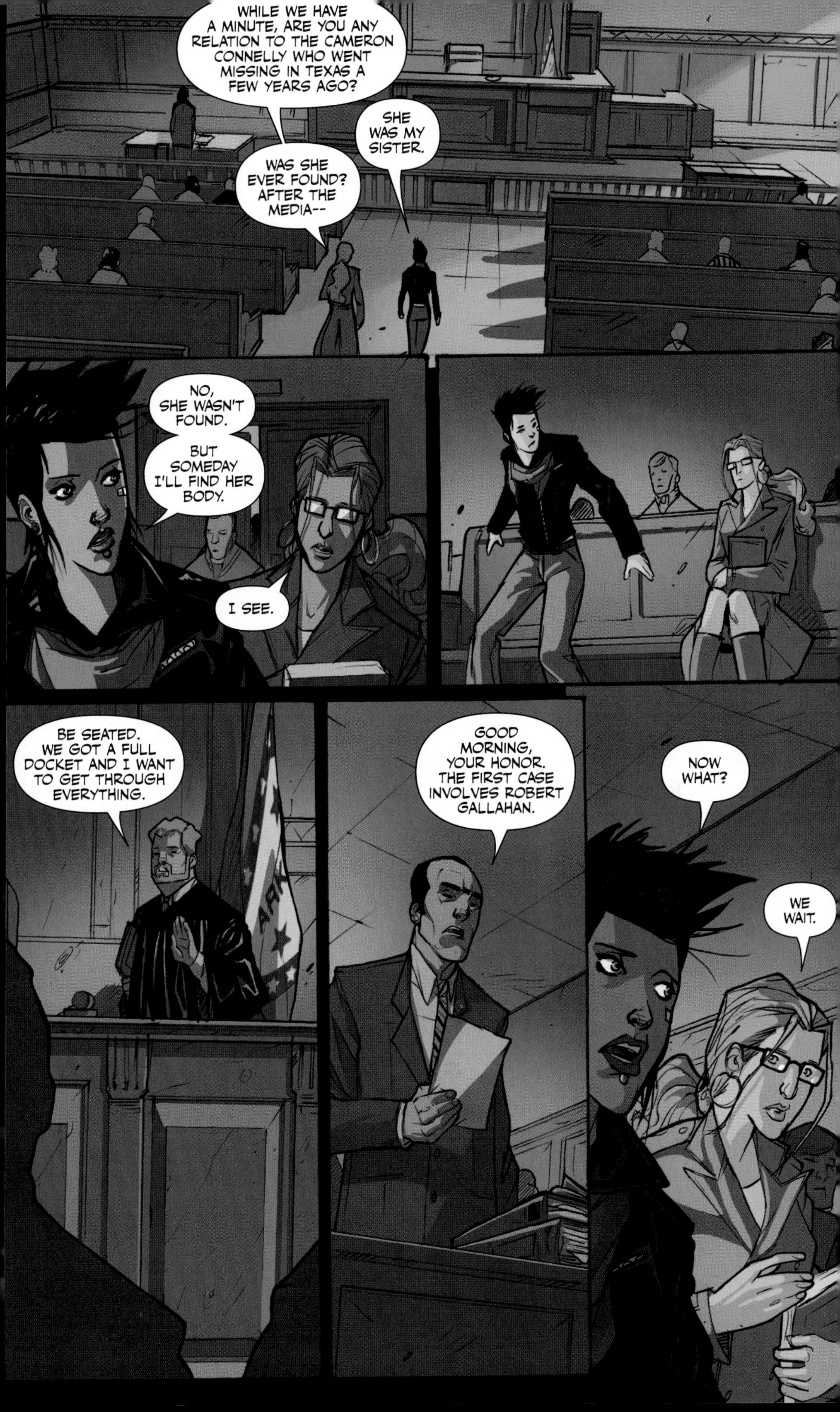
WHILE WE HAVE A MINUTE, ARE YOU ANY RELATION TO THE CAMERON CONNELLY WHO WENT MISSING IN TEXAS A FEW YEARS AGO?
SHE WAS MY SISTER.
WAS SHE EVER FOUND? AFTER THE MEDIA--
NO, SHE WASN'T FOUND.
BUT SOMEDAY I'LL FIND HER BODY.
I SEE.
BE SEATED. WE GOT A FULL DOCKET AND I WANT TO GET THROUGH EVERYTHING.
GOOD MORNING, YOUR HONOR. THE FIRST CASE INVOLVES ROBERT GALLAHAN.
NOW WHAT?
WE WAIT.

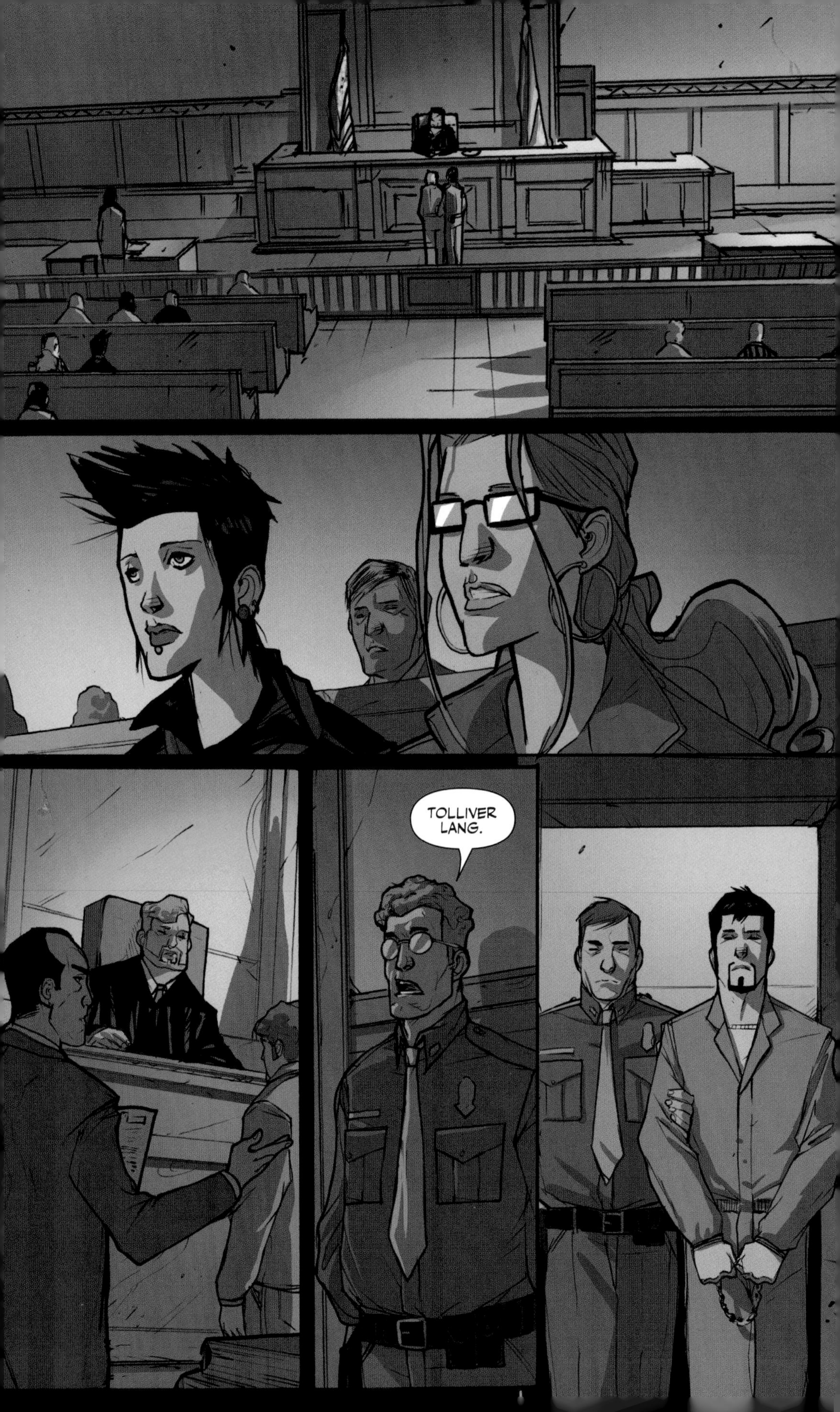
TOLLIVER LANG.

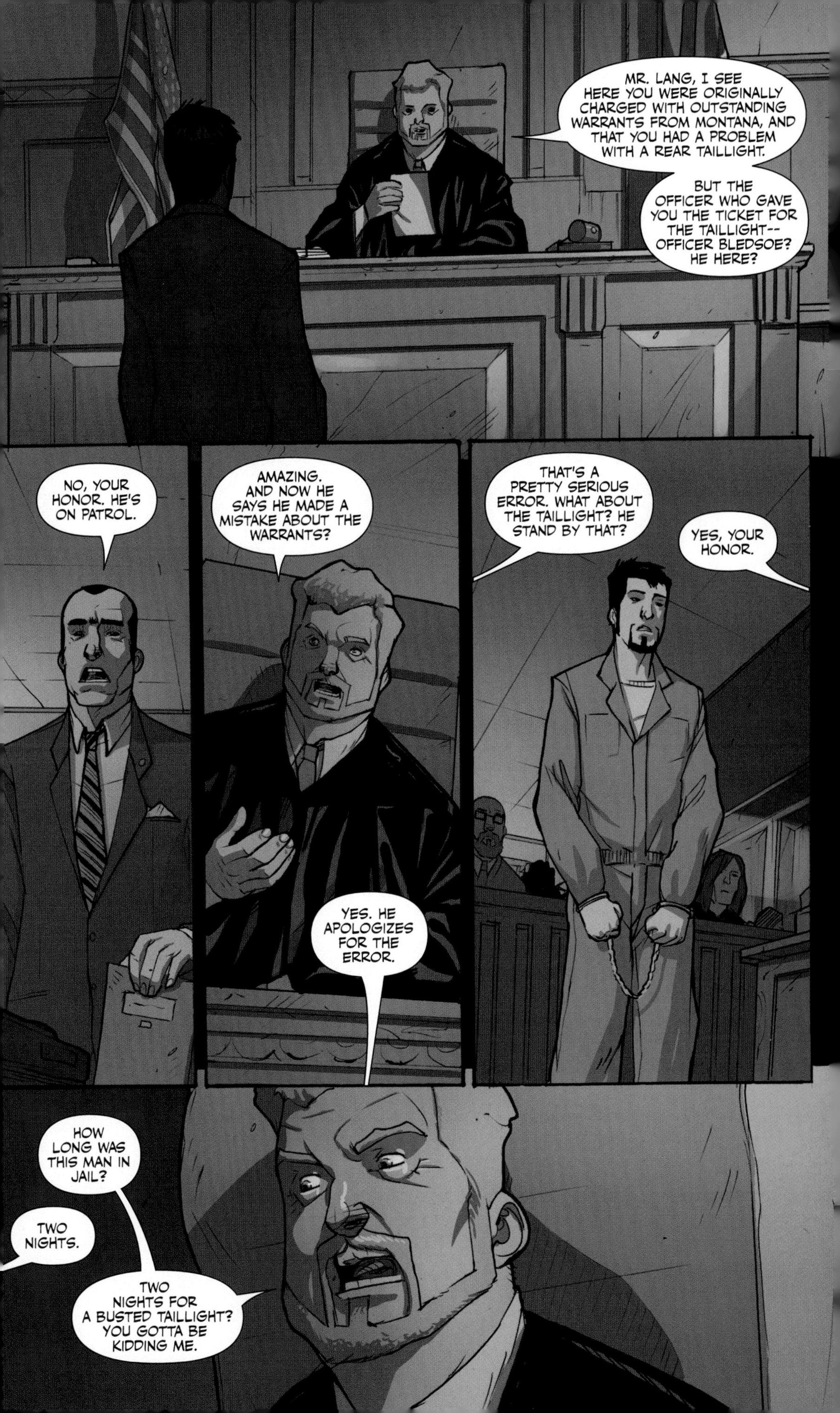
MR. LANG, I SEE HERE YOU WERE ORIGINALLY CHARGED WITH OUTSTANDING WARRANTS FROM MONTANA, AND THAT YOU HAD A PROBLEM WITH A REAR TAILLIGHT.
BUT THE OFFICER WHO GAVE YOU THE TICKET FOR THE TAILLIGHT-- OFFICER BLEDSOE? HE HERE?
NO, YOUR HONOR. HE'S ON PATROL.
AMAZING. AND NOW HE SAYS HE MADE A MISTAKE ABOUT THE WARRANTS?
YES. HE APOLOGIZES FOR THE ERROR.
THAT'S A PRETTY SERIOUS ERROR. WHAT ABOUT THE TAILLIGHT? HE STAND BY THAT?
YES, YOUR HONOR.
HOW LONG WAS THIS MAN IN JAIL?
TWO NIGHTS.
TWO NIGHTS FOR A BUSTED TAILLIGHT? YOU GOTTA BE KIDDING ME.

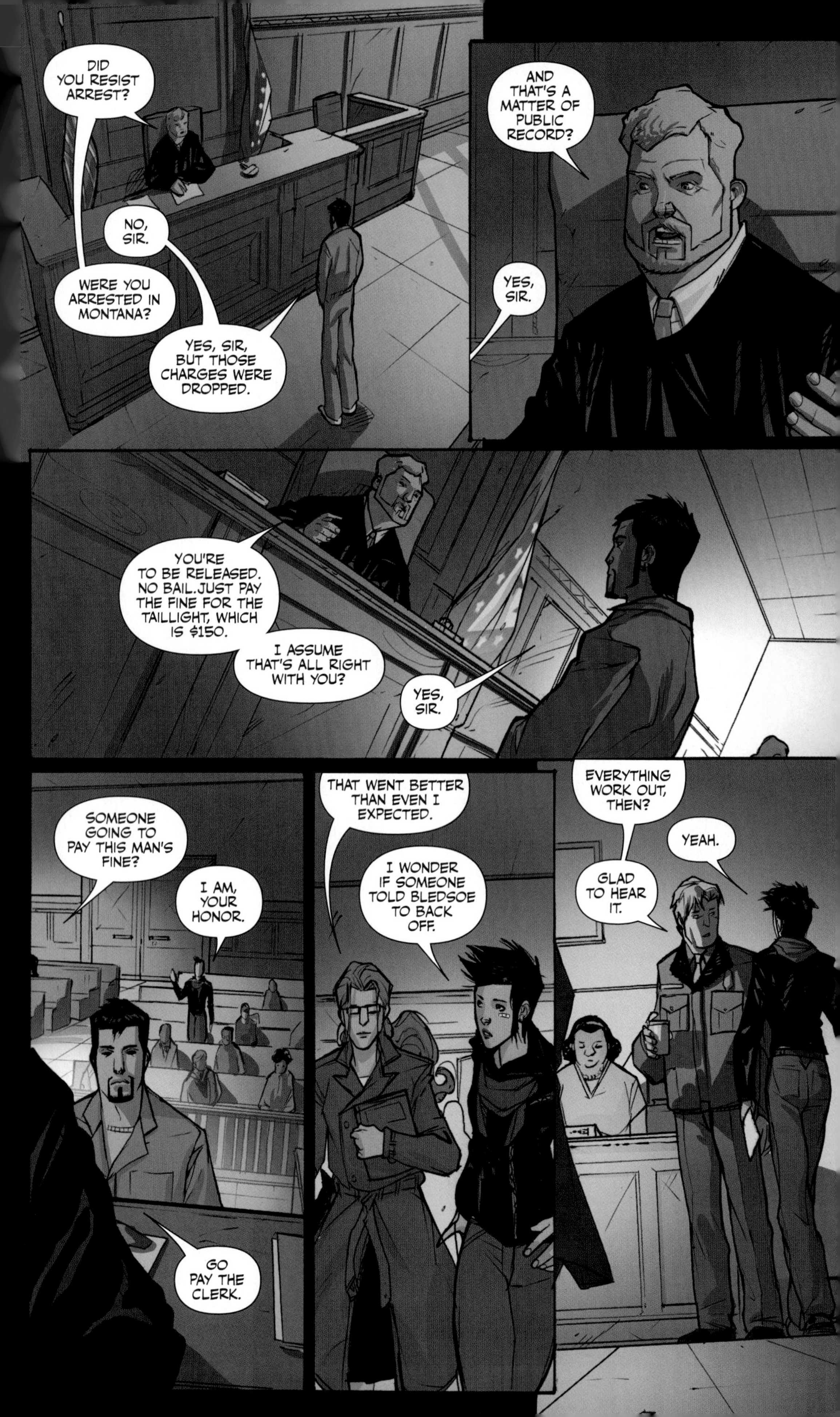
DID YOU RESIST ARREST?
NO, SIR.
WERE YOU ARRESTED IN MONTANA?
YES, SIR, BUT THOSE CHARGES WERE DROPPED.
AND THAT'S A MATTER OF PUBLIC RECORD?
YES, SIR.
YOU'RE TO BE RELEASED. NO BAIL.JUST PAY THE FINE FOR THE TAILLIGHT, WHICH IS $150.
I ASSUME THAT'S ALL RIGHT WITH YOU?
YES, SIR.
SOMEONE GOING TO PAY THIS MAN'S FINE?
I AM, YOUR HONOR.
GO PAY THE CLERK.
THAT WENT BETTER THAN EVEN I EXPECTED.
I WONDER IF SOMEONE TOLD BLEDSOE TO BACK OFF.
EVERYTHING WORK OUT, THEN?
YEAH.
GLAD TO HEAR IT.

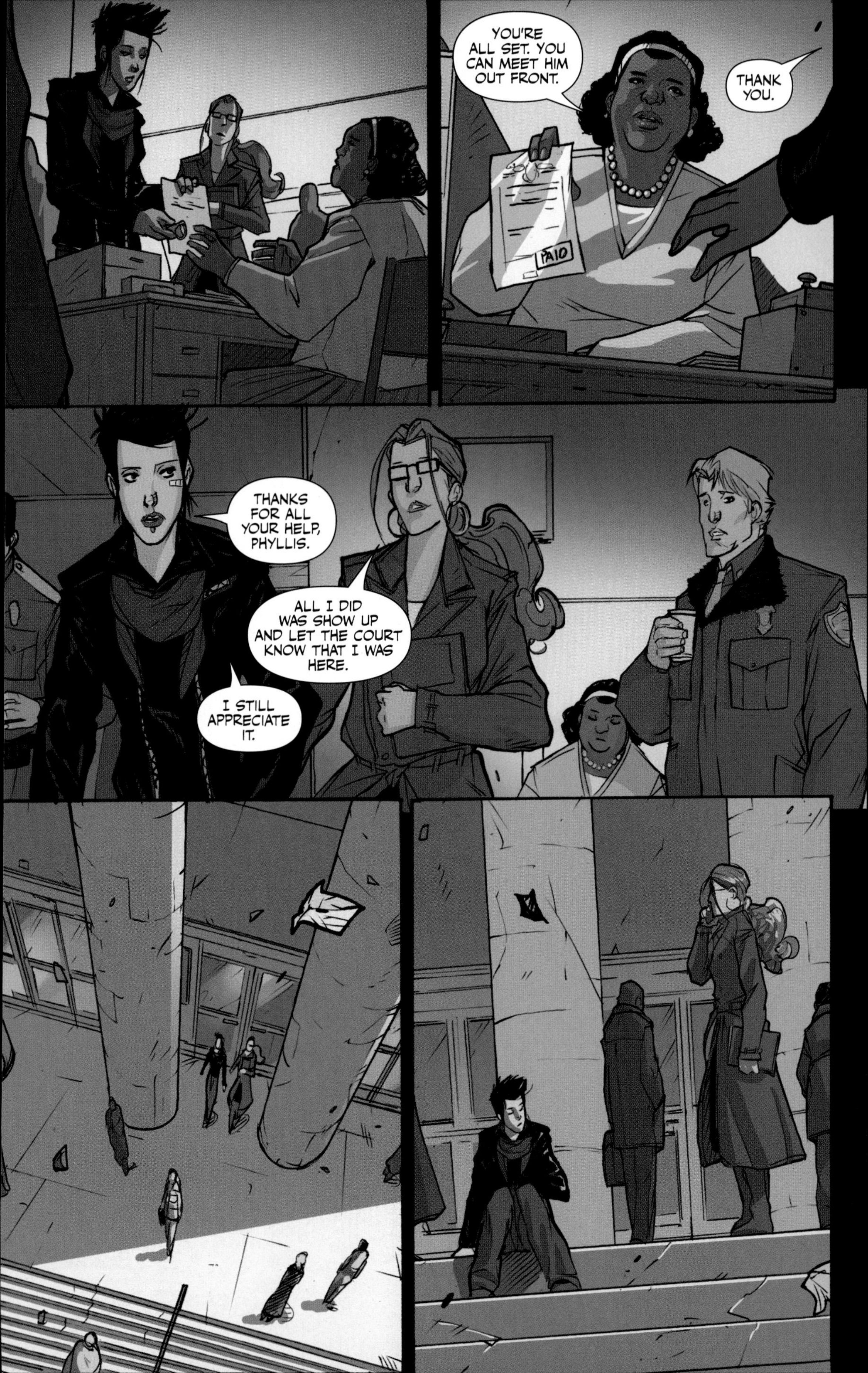
YOU'RE ALL SET. YOU CAN MEET HIM OUT FRONT.
THANK YOU.
PA10
THANKS FOR ALL YOUR HELP, PHYLLIS.
ALL I DID WAS SHOW UP AND LET THE COURT KNOW THAT I WAS HERE.
I STILL APPRECIATE IT.

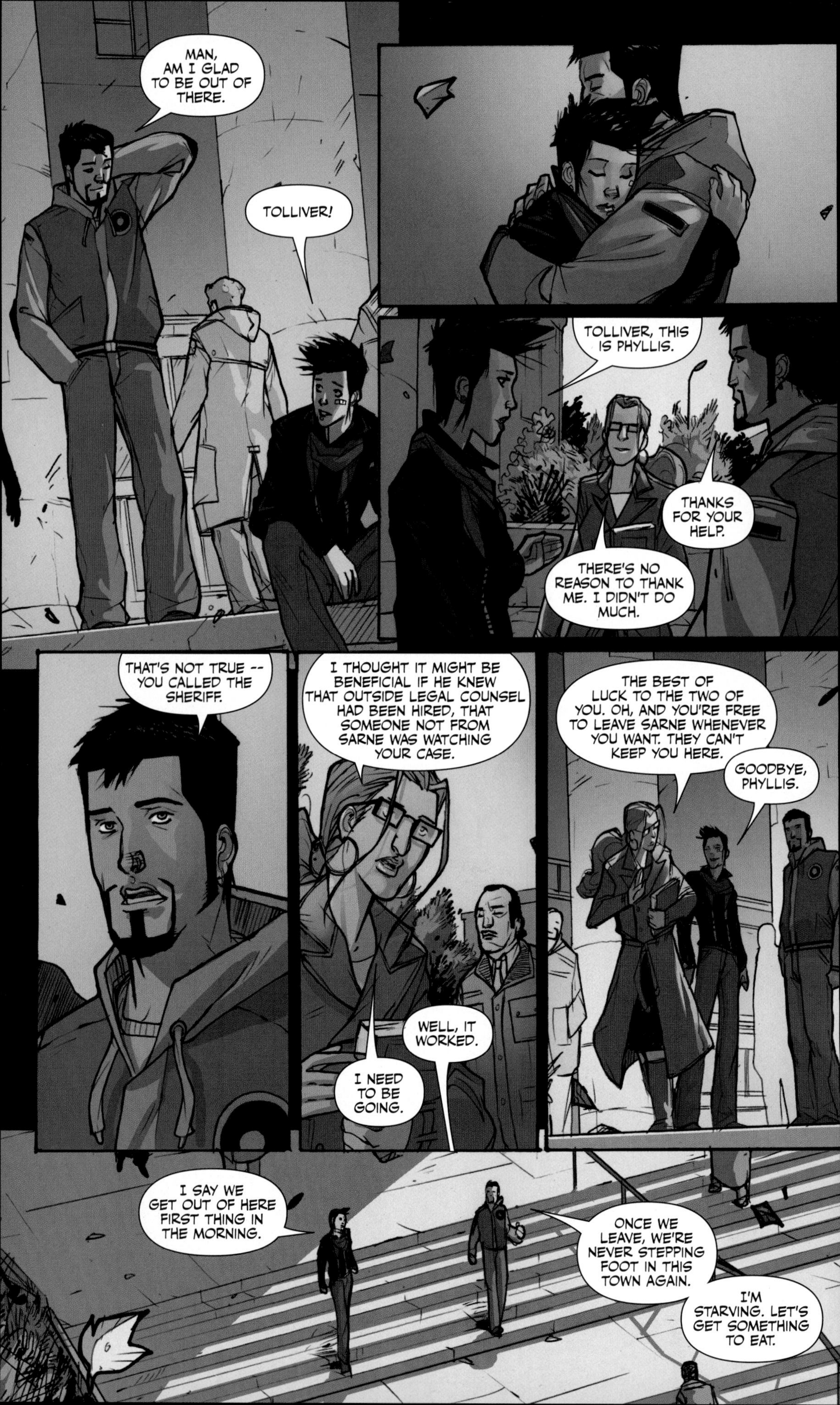
MAN, AM I GLAD TO BE OUT OF THERE.
TOLLIVER!
TOLLIVER, THIS IS PHYLLIS.
THANKS FOR YOUR HELP.
THERE'S NO REASON TO THANK ME. I DIDN'T DO MUCH.
THAT'S NOT TRUE -- YOU CALLED THE SHERIFF.
I THOUGHT IT MIGHT BE BENEFICIAL IF HE KNEW THAT OUTSIDE LEGAL COUNSEL HAD BEEN HIRED, THAT SOMEONE NOT FROM SARNE WAS WATCHING YOUR CASE.
WELL, IT WORKED.
I NEED TO BE GOING.
THE BEST OF LUCK TO THE TWO OF YOU. OH, AND YOU'RE FREE TO LEAVE SARNE WHENEVER YOU WANT. THEY CAN'T KEEP YOU HERE.
GOODBYE, PHYLLIS.
I SAY WE GET OUT OF HERE FIRST THING IN THE MORNING.
ONCE WE LEAVE, WE'RE NEVER STEPPING FOOT IN THIS TOWN AGAIN.
I'M STARVING. LET'S GET SOMETHING TO EAT.

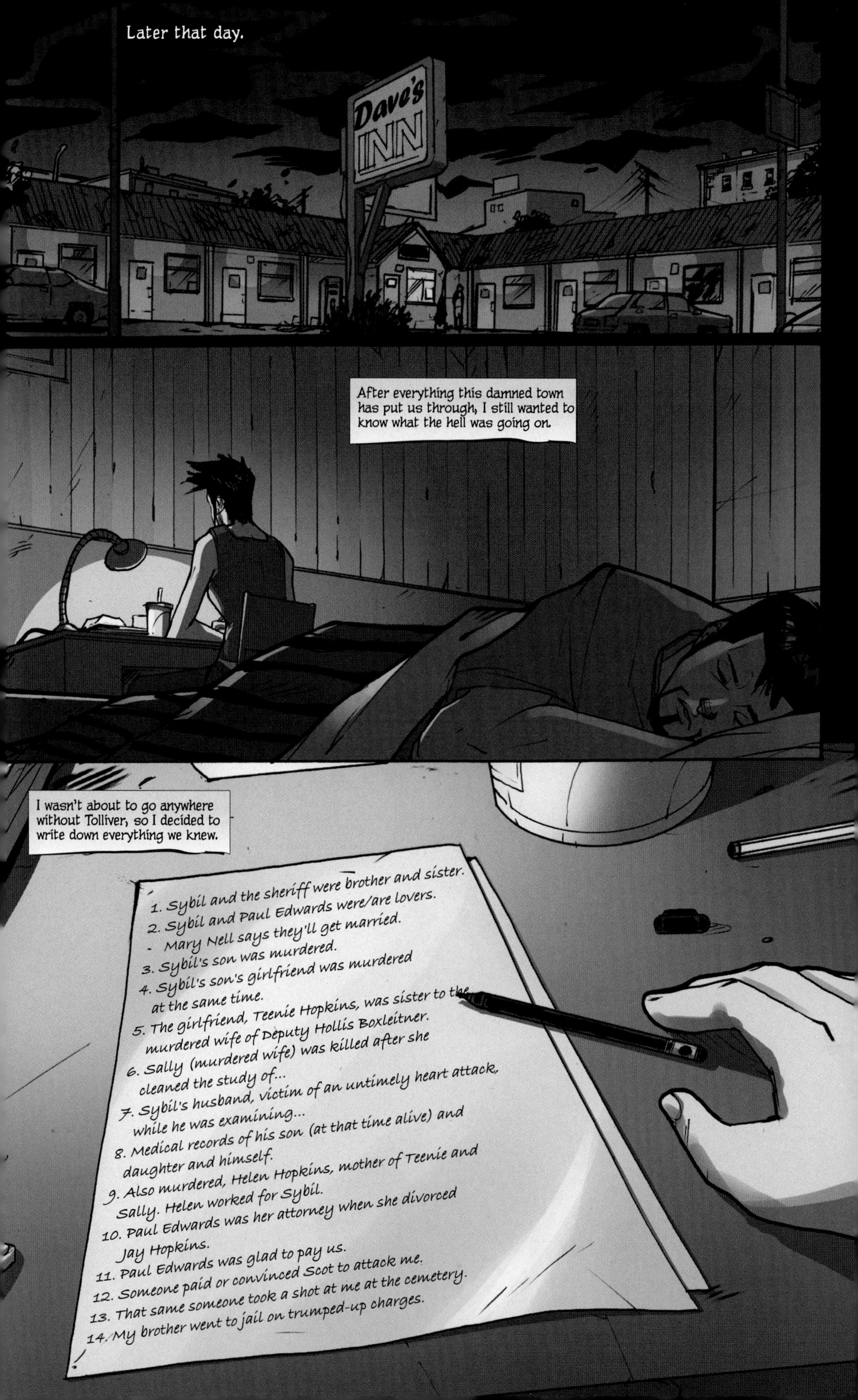
Later that day.
Dave's INN
After everything this damned town has put us through, I still wanted to know what the hell was going on.
I wasn't about to go anywhere without Tolliver, so I decided to write down everything we knew.
1. Sybil and the sheriff were brother and sister.
2. Sybil and Paul Edwards were/are lovers.
- Mary Nell says they'll get married.
3. Sybil's son was murdered.
4. Sybil's son's girlfriend was murdered at the same time.
5. The girlfriend, Teenie Hopkins, was sister to the murdered wife of Deputy Hollis Boxleitner.
6. Sally (murdered wife) was killed after she cleaned the study of...
7. Sybil's husband, victim of an untimely heart attack, while he was examining...
8. Medical records of his son (at that time alive) and daughter and himself.
9. Also murdered, Helen Hopkins, mother of Teenie and Sally. Helen worked for Sybil.
10. Paul Edwards was her attorney when she divorced Jay Hopkins.
11. Paul Edwards was glad to pay us.
12. Someone paid or convinced Scot to attack me.
13. That same someone took a shot at me at the cemetery.
14. My brother went to jail on trumped-up charges.

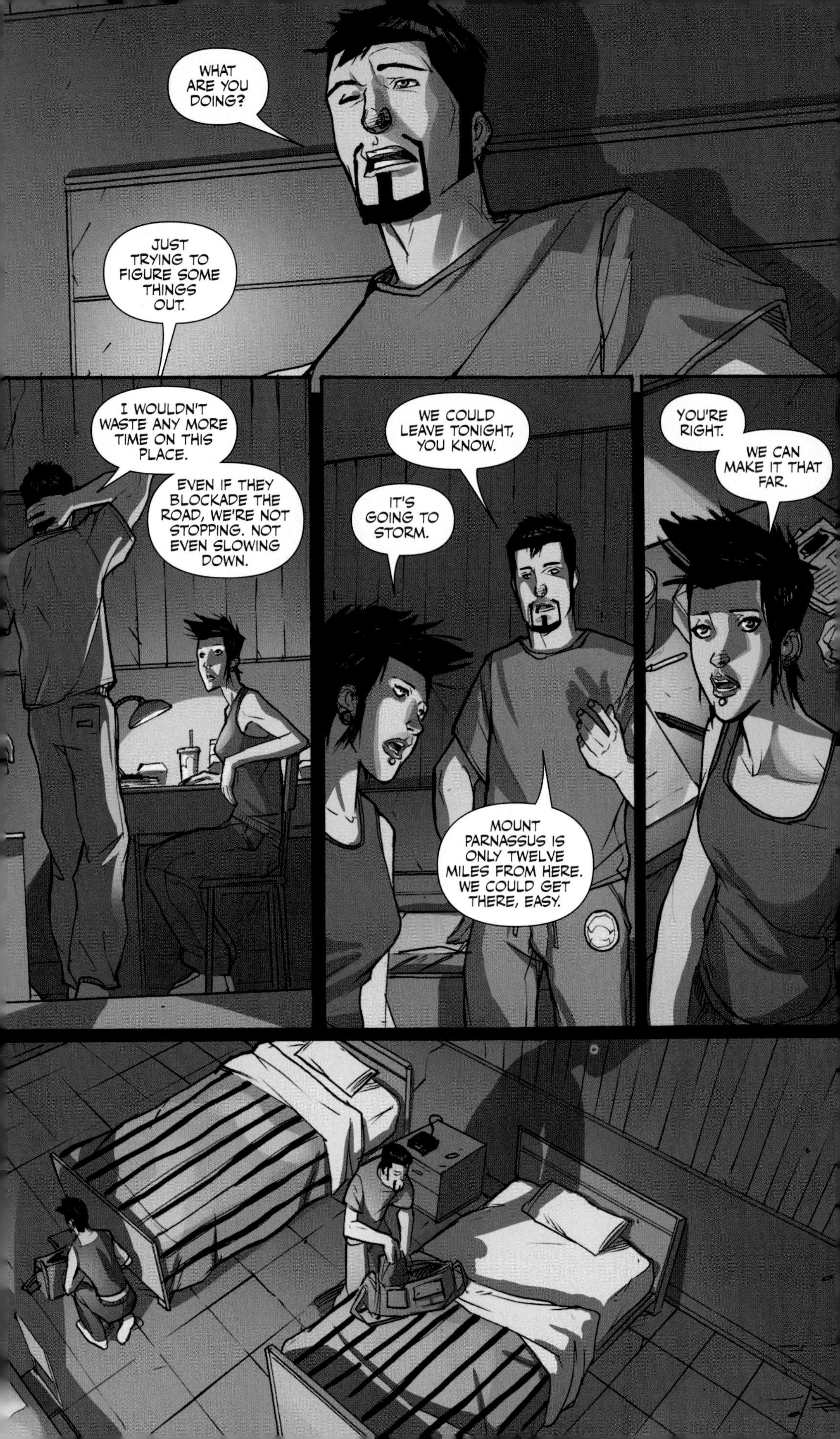
WHAT ARE YOU DOING?
JUST TRYING TO FIGURE SOME THINGS OUT.
I WOULDN'T WASTE ANY MORE TIME ON THIS PLACE.
EVEN IF THEY BLOCKADE THE ROAD, WE'RE NOT STOPPING. NOT EVEN SLOWING DOWN.
WE COULD LEAVE TONIGHT, YOU KNOW.
IT'S GOING TO STORM.
MOUNT PARNASSUS IS ONLY TWELVE MILES FROM HERE. WE COULD GET THERE, EASY.
YOU'RE RIGHT.
WE CAN MAKE IT THAT FAR.

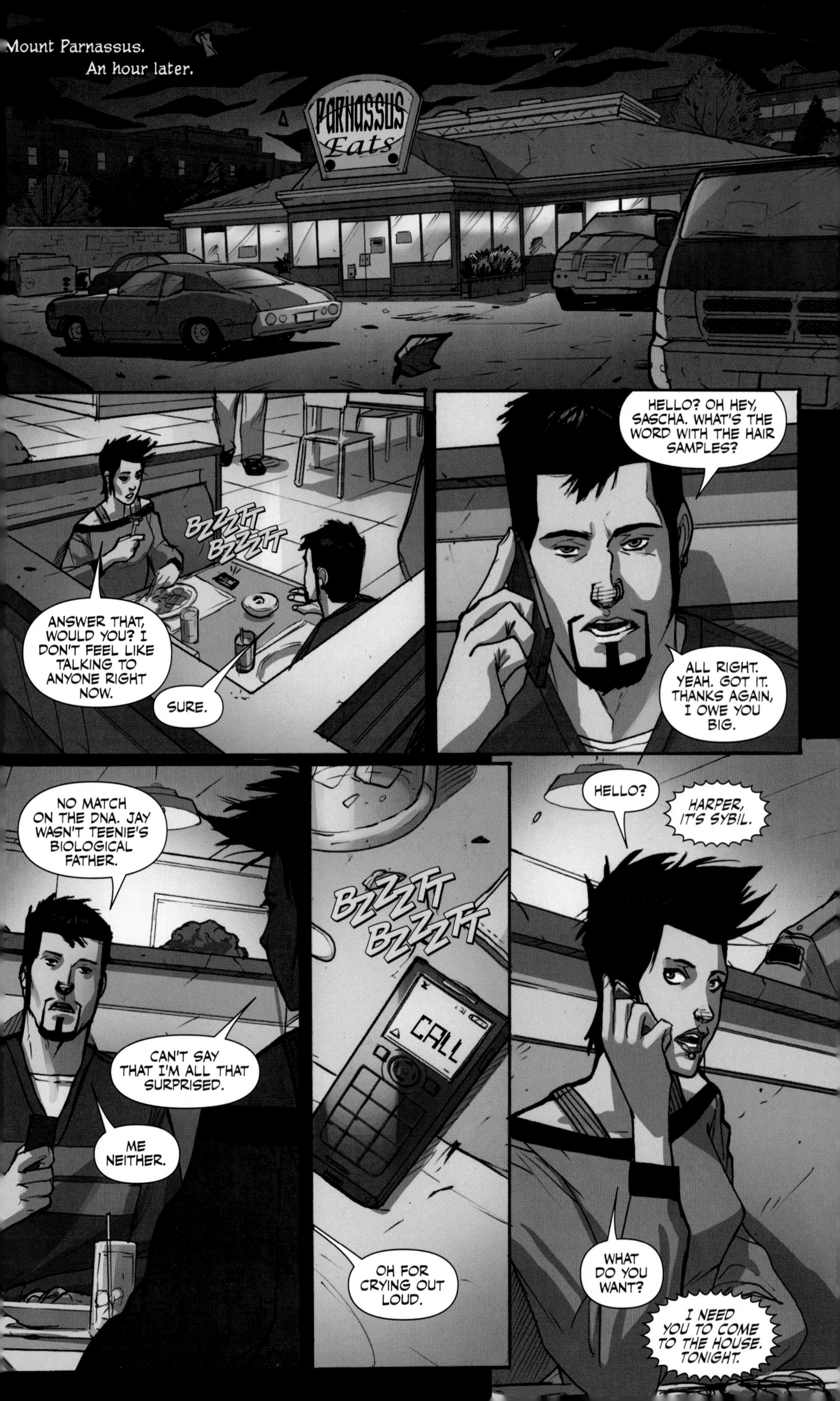

Mount Parnassus.
An hour later.
PARNASSUS Eats
BZZZFT BZZZFT
ANSWER THAT, WOULD YOU? I DON'T FEEL LIKE TALKING TO ANYONE RIGHT NOW.
SURE.
HELLO? OH HEY, SASCHA. WHAT'S THE WORD WITH THE HAIR SAMPLES?
ALL RIGHT. YEAH. GOT IT. THANKS AGAIN, I OWE YOU BIG.
NO MATCH ON THE DNA. JAY WASN'T TEENIE'S BIOLOGICAL FATHER.
CAN'T SAY THAT I'M ALL THAT SURPRISED.
ME NEITHER.
BZZZFT BZZZFT
CALL
OH FOR CRYING OUT LOUD.
HELLO?
HARPER, IT'S SYBIL.
WHAT DO YOU WANT?
I NEED YOU TO COME TO THE HOUSE. TONIGHT.

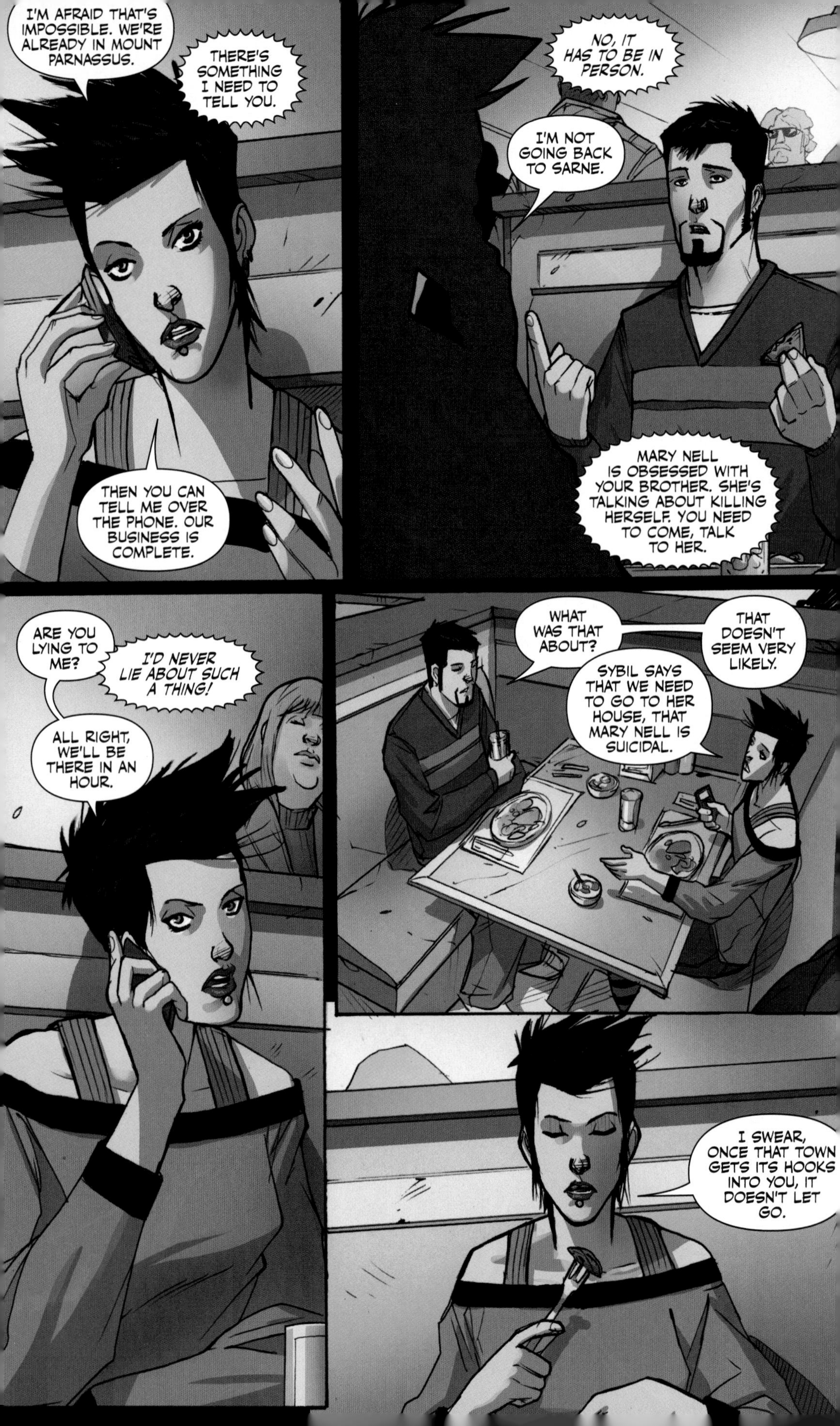
I'M AFRAID THAT'S IMPOSSIBLE. WE'RE ALREADY IN MOUNT PARNASSUS.
THERE'S SOMETHING I NEED TO TELL YOU.
THEN YOU CAN TELL ME OVER THE PHONE. OUR BUSINESS IS COMPLETE.
NO, IT HAS TO BE IN PERSON.
I'M NOT GOING BACK TO SARNE.
MARY NELL IS OBSESSED WITH YOUR BROTHER. SHE'S TALKING ABOUT KILLING HERSELF. YOU NEED TO COME, TALK TO HER.
ARE YOU LYING TO ME?
I'D NEVER LIE ABOUT SUCH A THING!
ALL RIGHT, WE'LL BE THERE IN AN HOUR.
WHAT WAS THAT ABOUT?
SYBIL SAYS THAT WE NEED TO GO TO HER HOUSE, THAT MARY NELL IS SUICIDAL.
THAT DOESN'T SEEM VERY LIKELY.
I SWEAR, ONCE THAT TOWN GETS ITS HOOKS INTO YOU, IT DOESN'T LET GO.

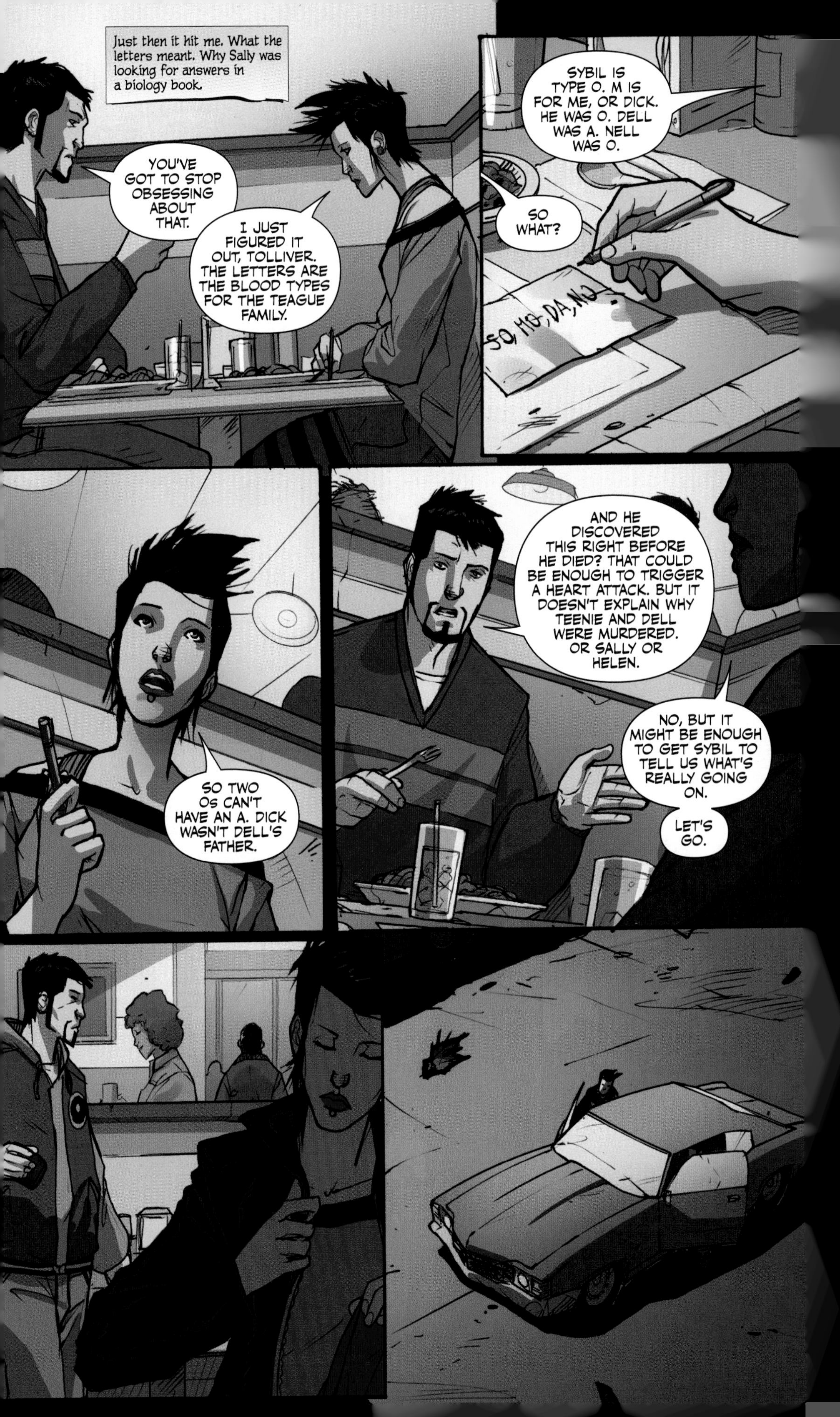
Just then it hit me. What the letters meant. Why Sally was looking for answers in a biology book.
YOU'VE GOT TO STOP OBSESSING ABOUT THAT.
I JUST FIGURED IT OUT, TOLLIVER. THE LETTERS ARE THE BLOOD TYPES FOR THE TEAGUE FAMILY.
SYBIL IS TYPE O. M IS FOR ME, OR DICK. HE WAS O. DELL WAS A. NELL WAS O.
SO WHAT?
SO, MO, DA, NO
SO TWO Os CAN'T HAVE AN A. DICK WASN'T DELL'S FATHER.
AND HE DISCOVERED THIS RIGHT BEFORE HE DIED? THAT COULD BE ENOUGH TO TRIGGER A HEART ATTACK. BUT IT DOESN'T EXPLAIN WHY TEENIE AND DELL WERE MURDERED. OR SALLY OR HELEN.
NO, BUT IT MIGHT BE ENOUGH TO GET SYBIL TO TELL US WHAT'S REALLY GOING ON.
LET'S GO.

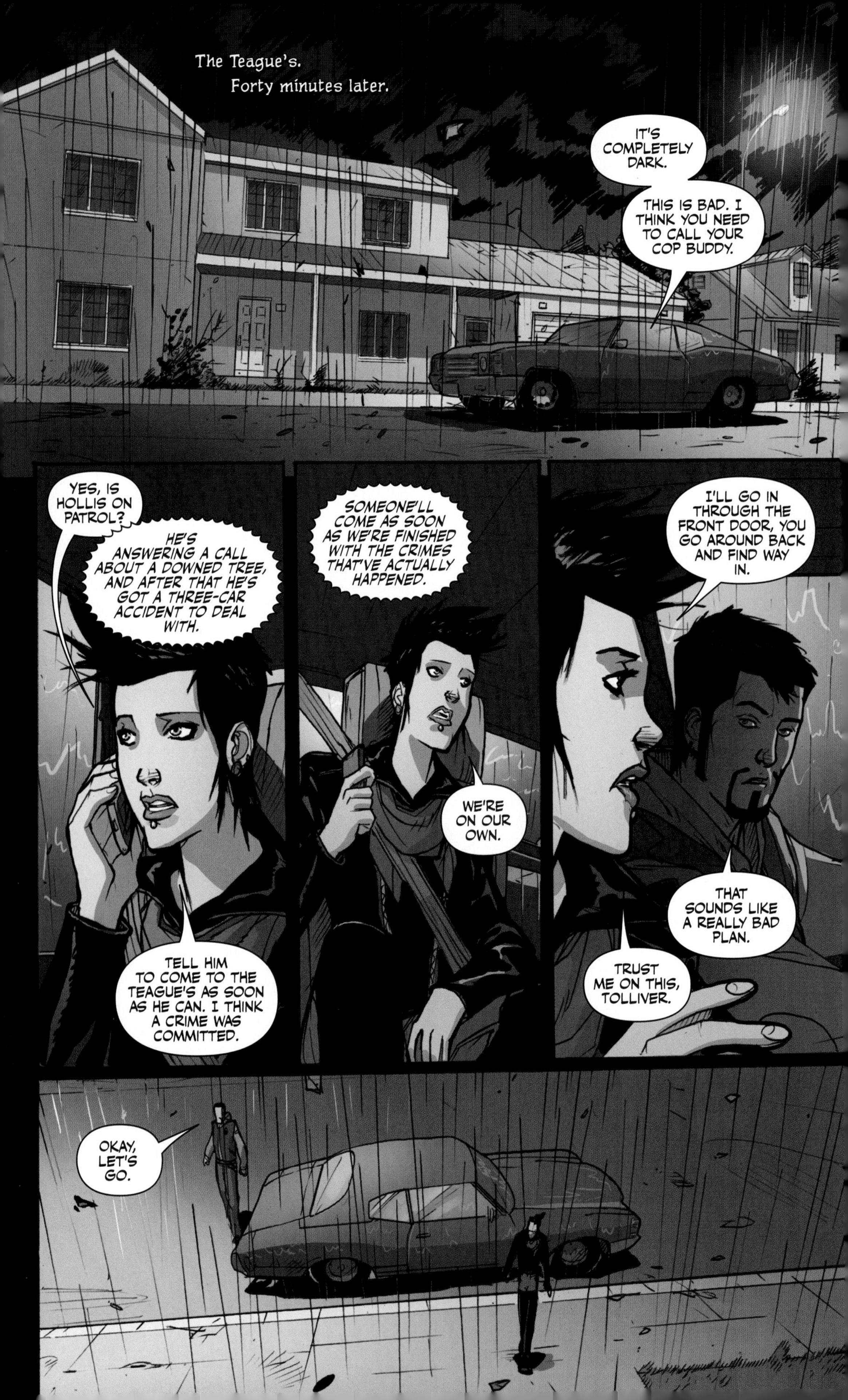

The Teague's.
Forty minutes later.
IT'S COMPLETELY DARK.
THIS IS BAD. I THINK YOU NEED TO CALL YOUR COP BUDDY.
YES, IS HOLLIS ON PATROL?
HE'S ANSWERING A CALL ABOUT A DOWNED TREE, AND AFTER THAT HE'S GOT A THREE-CAR ACCIDENT TO DEAL WITH.
TELL HIM TO COME TO THE TEAGUE'S AS SOON AS HE CAN. I THINK A CRIME WAS COMMITTED.
SOMEONE'LL COME AS SOON AS WE'RE FINISHED WITH THE CRIMES THAT'VE ACTUALLY HAPPENED.
WE'RE ON OUR OWN.
I'LL GO IN THROUGH THE FRONT DOOR, YOU GO AROUND BACK AND FIND WAY IN.
THAT SOUNDS LIKE A REALLY BAD PLAN.
TRUST ME ON THIS, TOLLIVER.
OKAY, LET'S GO.

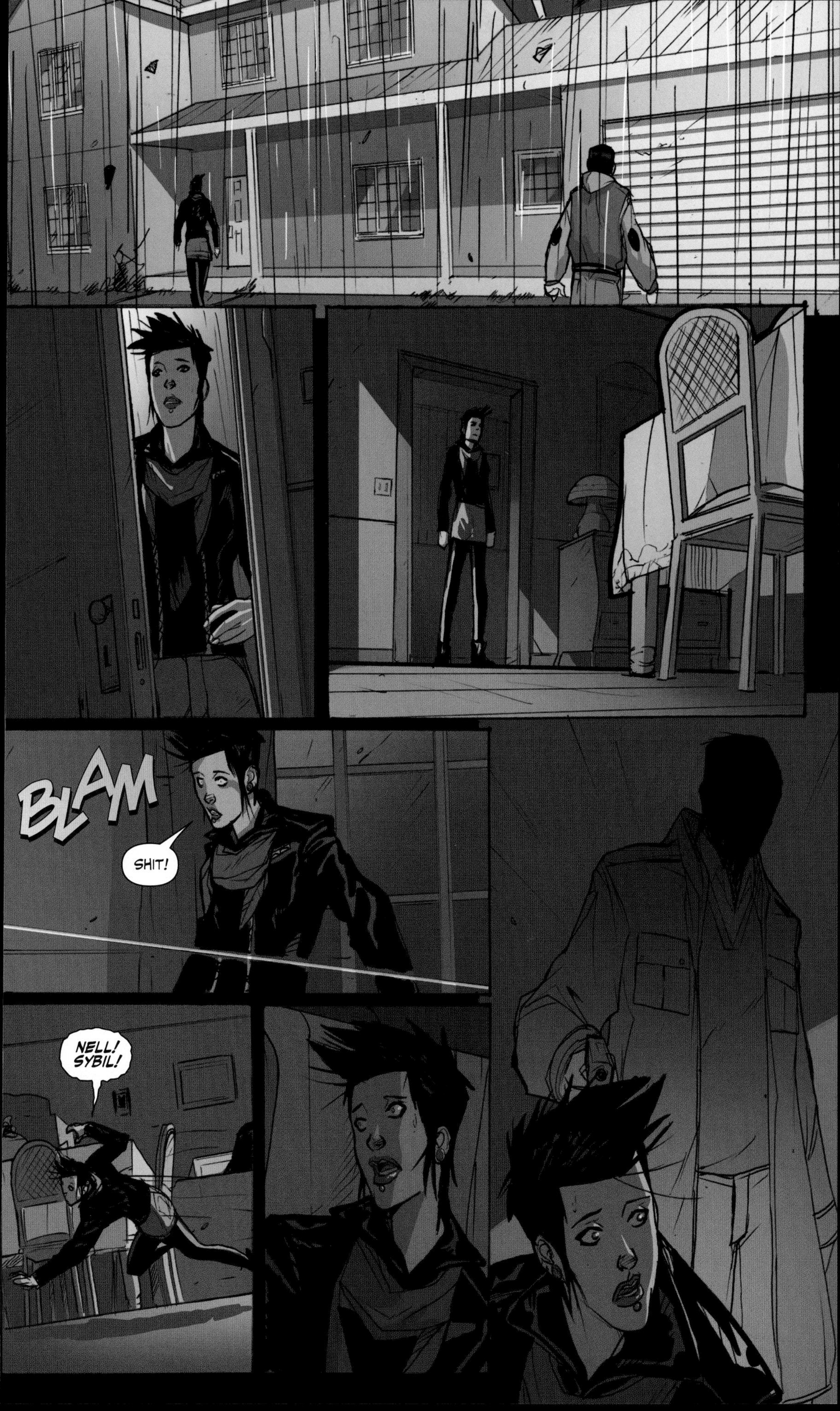
BLAM
SHIT!
NELL! SYBIL!

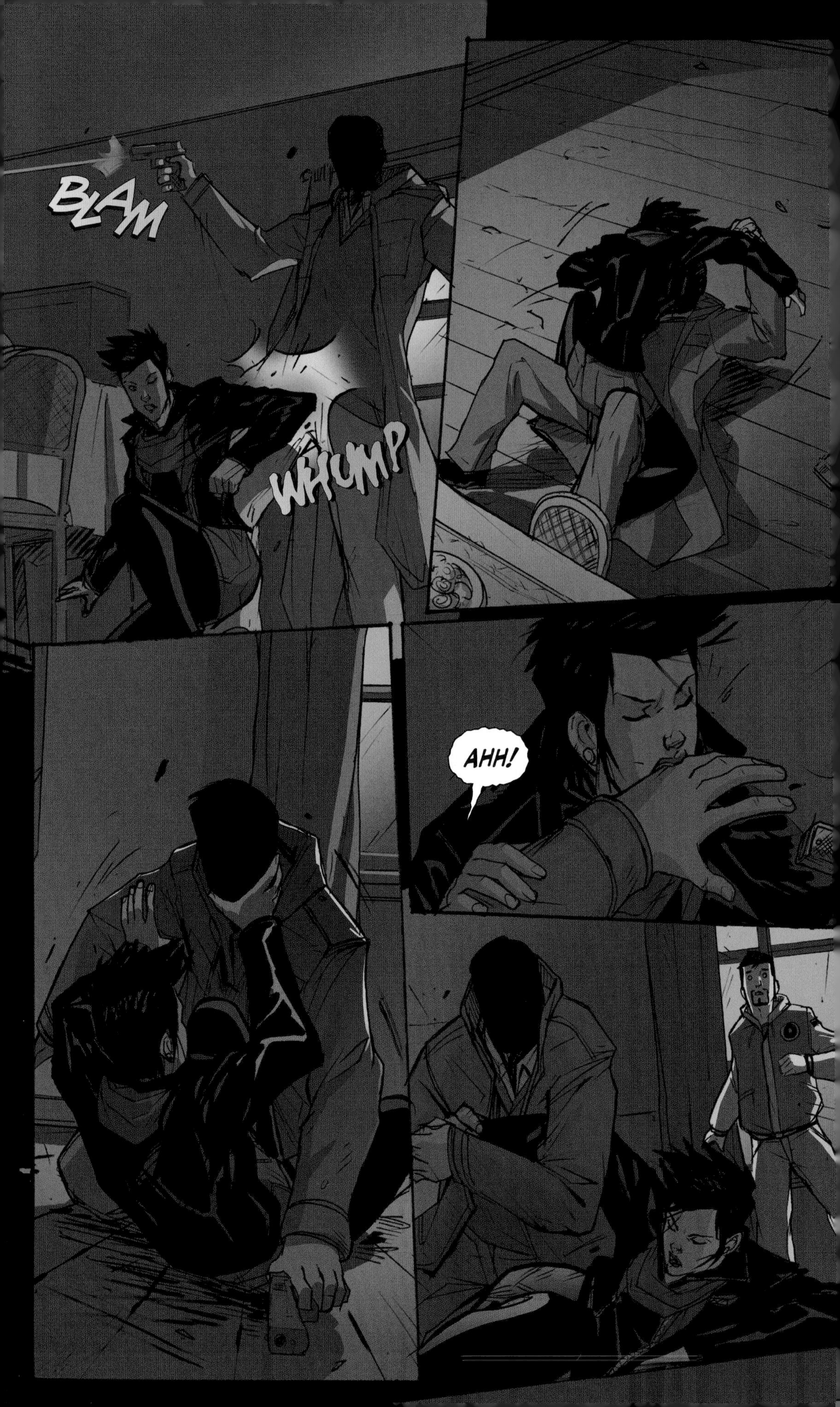
BLAM
WHUMP
AHH!

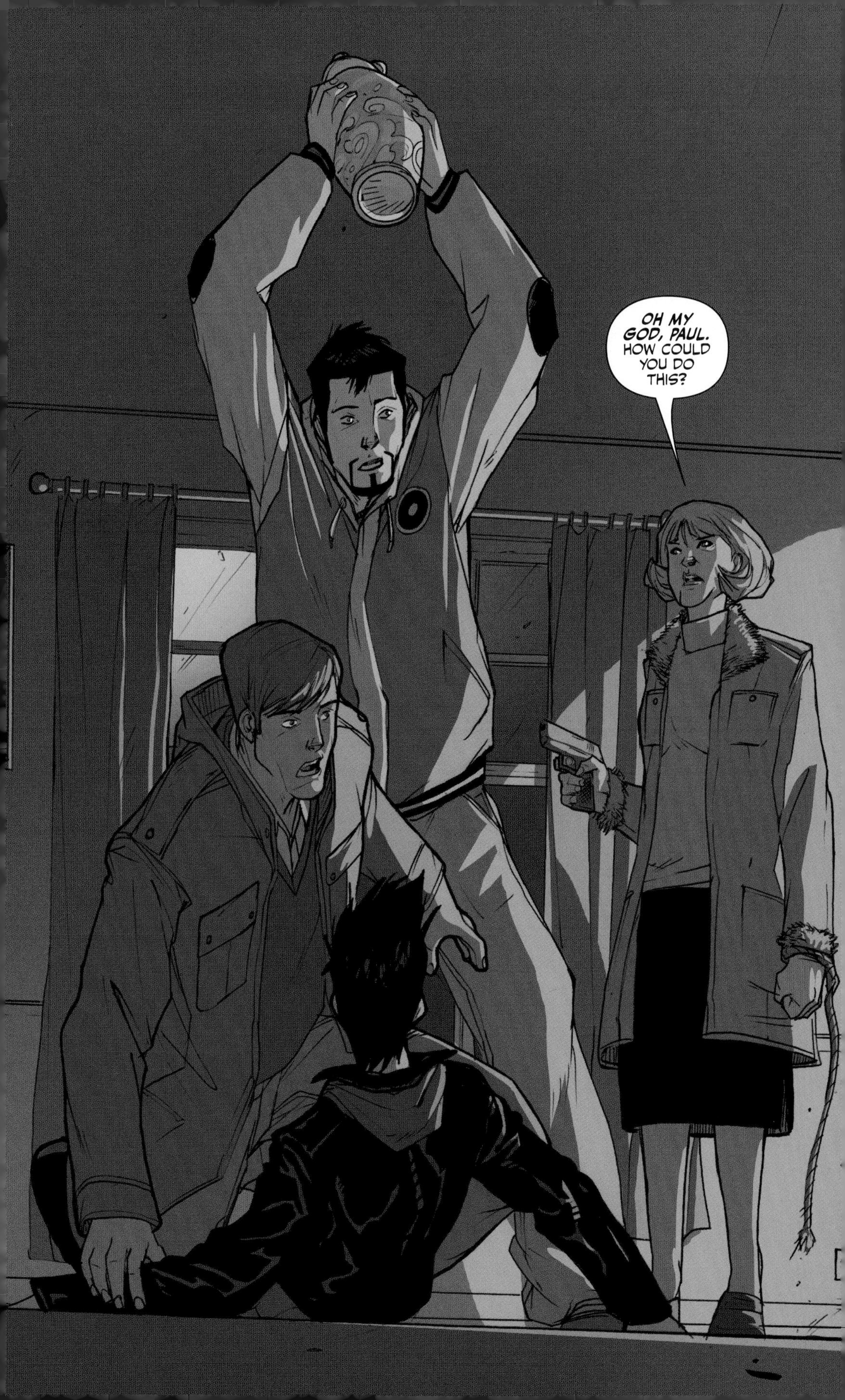
OH MY GOD, PAUL. HOW COULD YOU DO THIS?

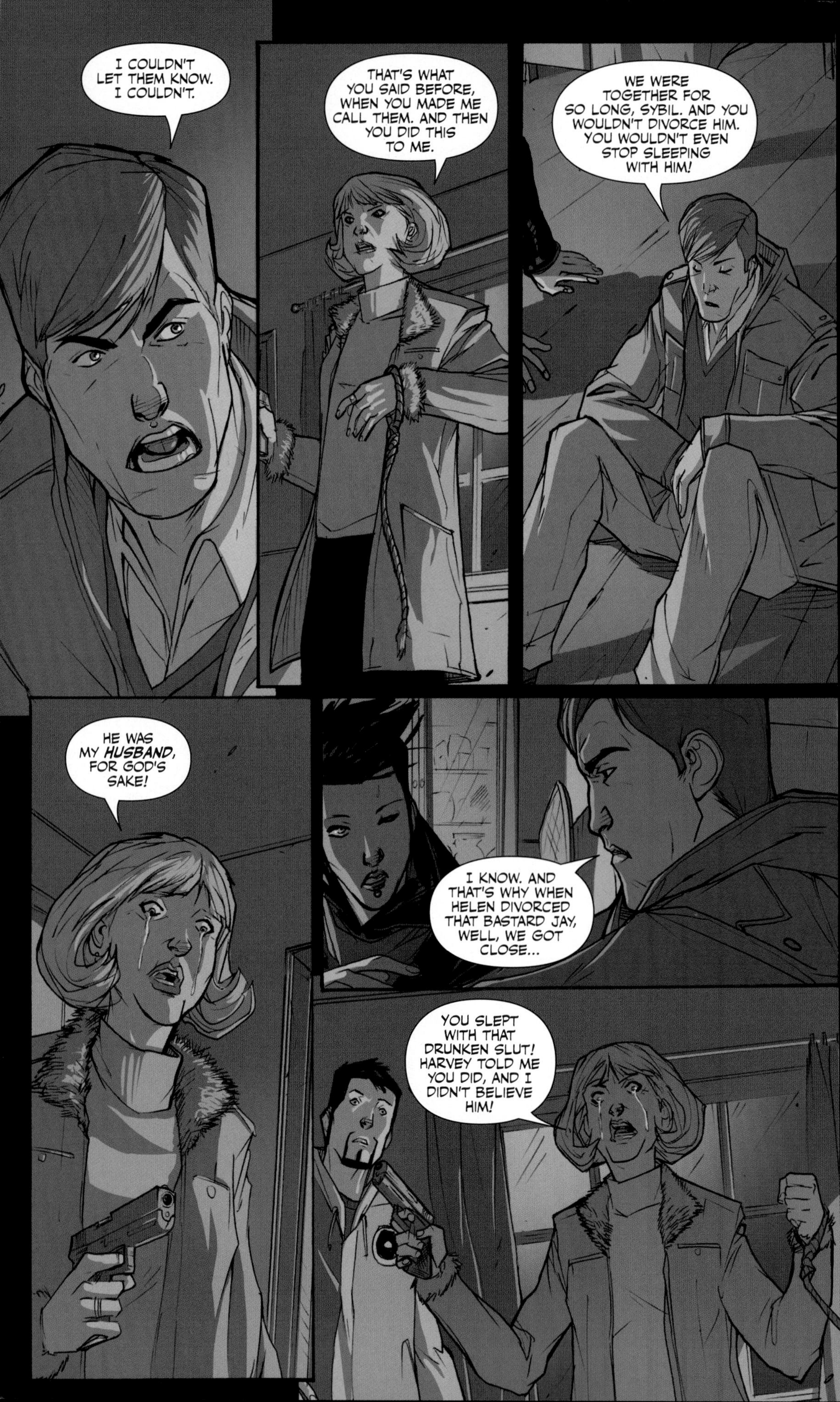

I COULDN'T LET THEM KNOW. I COULDN'T.
THAT'S WHAT YOU SAID BEFORE, WHEN YOU MADE ME CALL THEM. AND THEN YOU DID THIS TO ME.
WE WERE TOGETHER FOR SO LONG, SYBIL. AND YOU WOULDN'T DIVORCE HIM. YOU WOULDN'T EVEN STOP SLEEPING WITH HIM!
HE WAS MY *HUSBAND*, FOR GOD'S SAKE!
I KNOW. AND THAT'S WHY WHEN HELEN DIVORCED THAT BASTARD JAY, WELL, WE GOT CLOSE...
YOU SLEPT WITH THAT DRUNKEN SLUT! HARVEY TOLD ME YOU DID, AND I DIDN'T BELIEVE HIM!

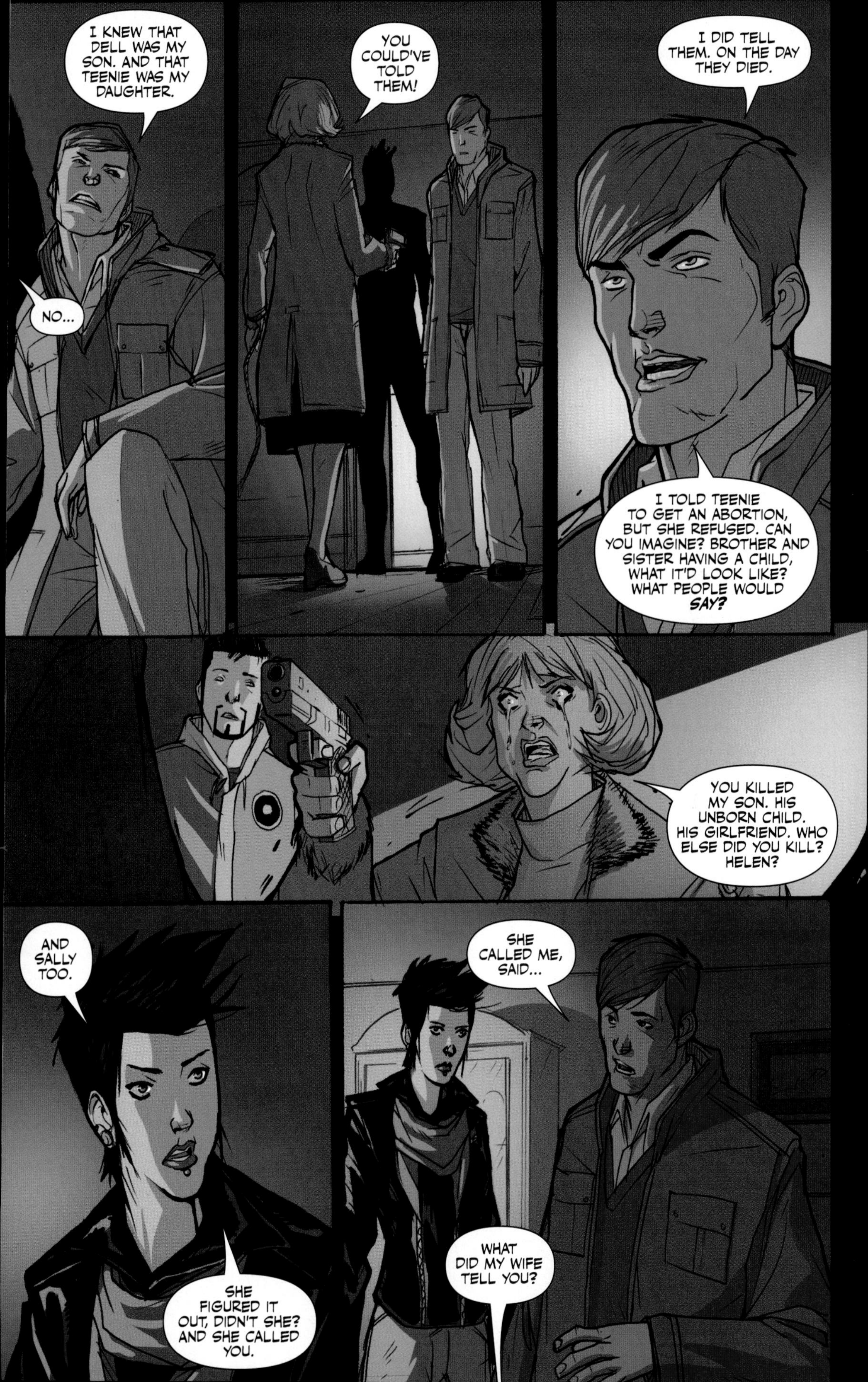
I KNEW THAT DELL WAS MY SON. AND THAT TEENIE WAS MY DAUGHTER.
NO...
YOU COULD'VE TOLD THEM!
I DID TELL THEM. ON THE DAY THEY DIED.
I TOLD TEENIE TO GET AN ABORTION, BUT SHE REFUSED. CAN YOU IMAGINE? BROTHER AND SISTER HAVING A CHILD, WHAT IT'D LOOK LIKE? WHAT PEOPLE WOULD *SAY?*
YOU KILLED MY SON. HIS UNBORN CHILD. HIS GIRLFRIEND. WHO ELSE DID YOU KILL? HELEN?
AND SALLY TOO.
SHE FIGURED IT OUT, DIDN'T SHE? AND SHE CALLED YOU.
SHE CALLED ME, SAID...
WHAT DID MY WIFE TELL YOU?

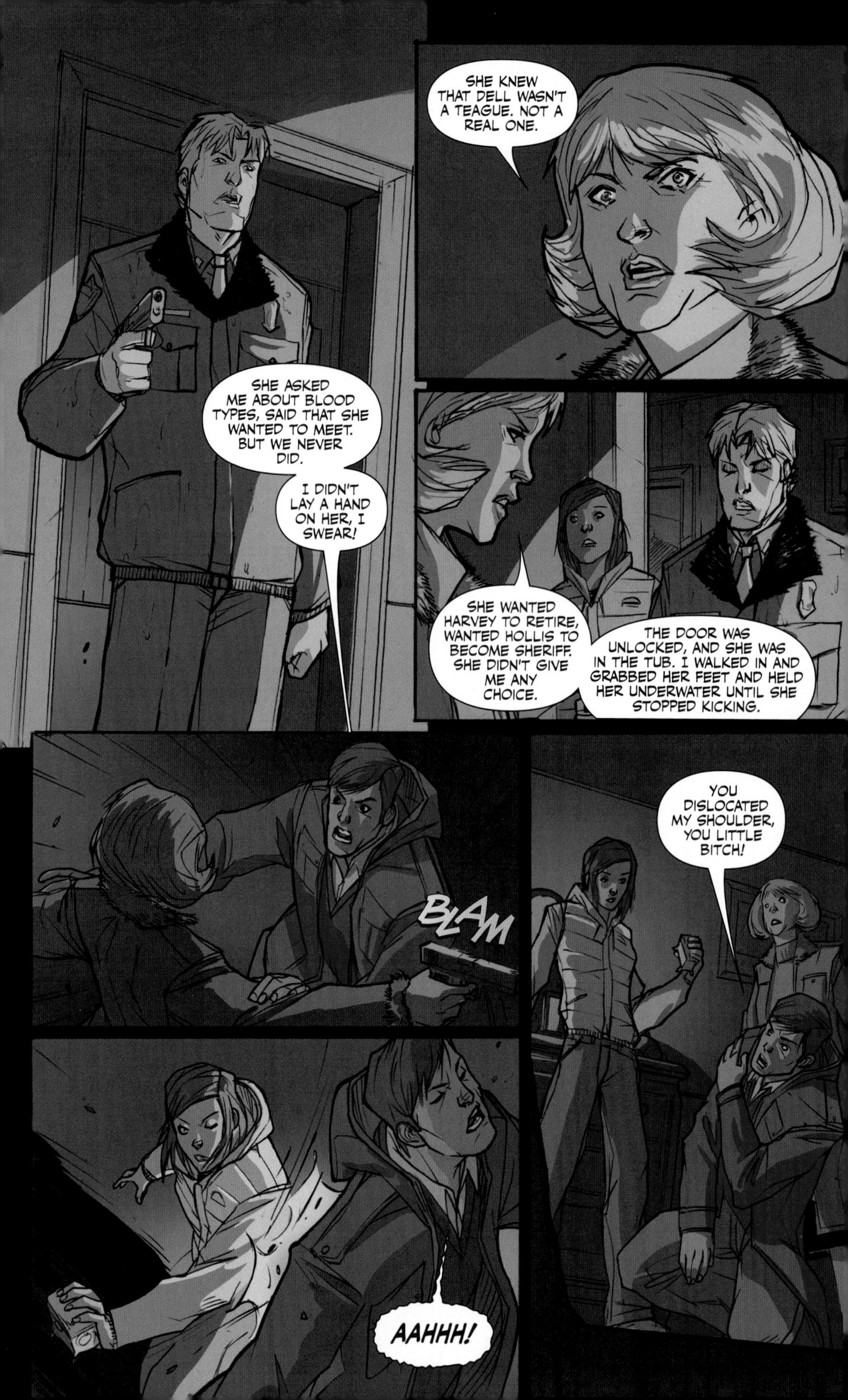
SHE KNEW THAT DELL WASN'T A TEAGUE. NOT A REAL ONE.
SHE ASKED ME ABOUT BLOOD TYPES, SAID THAT SHE WANTED TO MEET. BUT WE NEVER DID.
I DIDN'T LAY A HAND ON HER, I SWEAR!
SHE WANTED HARVEY TO RETIRE, WANTED HOLLIS TO BECOME SHERIFF. SHE DIDN'T GIVE ME ANY CHOICE.
THE DOOR WAS UNLOCKED, AND SHE WAS IN THE TUB. I WALKED IN AND GRABBED HER FEET AND HELD HER UNDERWATER UNTIL SHE STOPPED KICKING.
BLAM
AAHHH!
YOU DISLOCATED MY SHOULDER, YOU LITTLE BITCH!

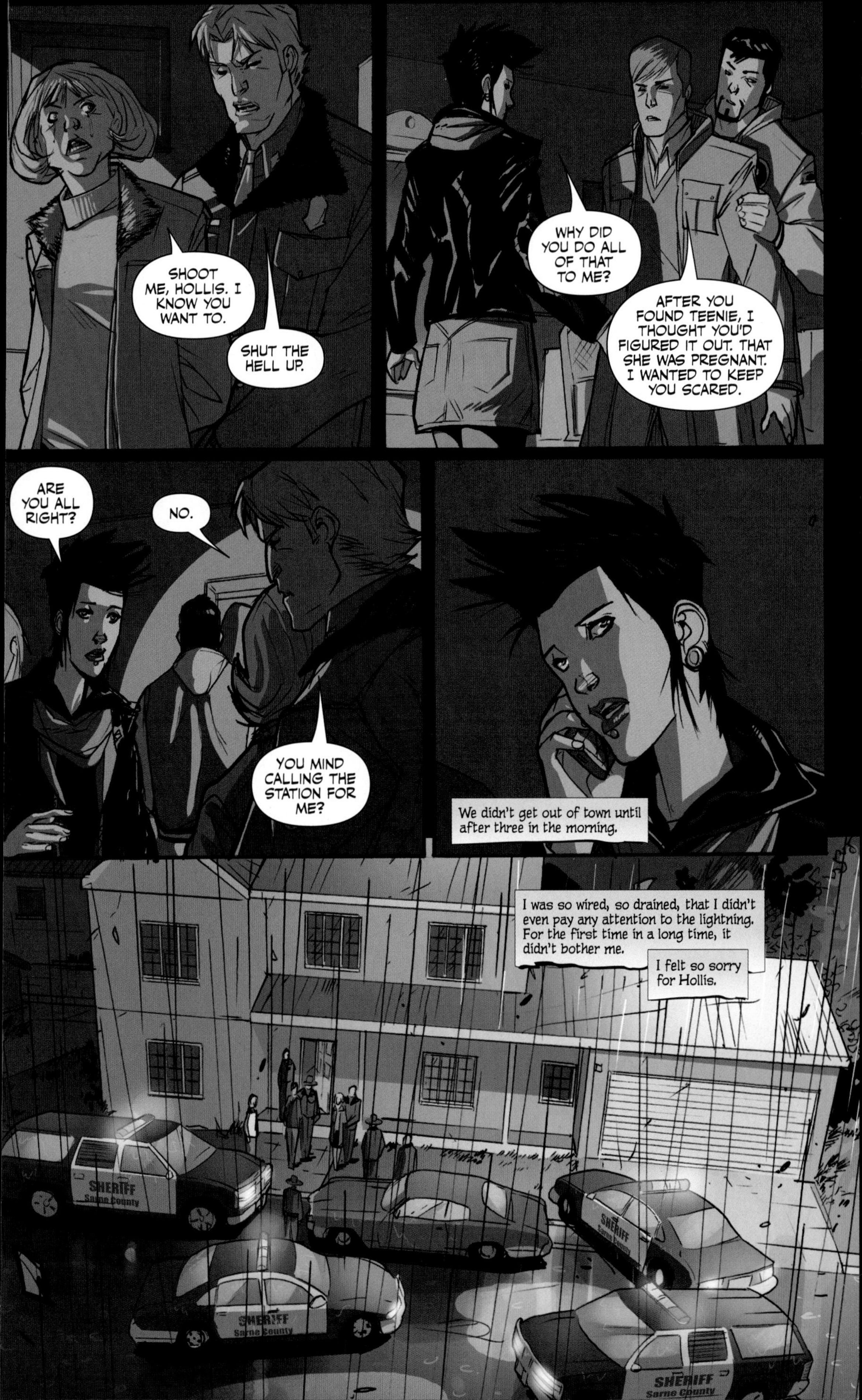
SHOOT ME, HOLLIS. I KNOW YOU WANT TO.
SHUT THE HELL UP.
WHY DID YOU DO ALL OF THAT TO ME?
AFTER YOU FOUND TEENIE, I THOUGHT YOU'D FIGURED IT OUT. THAT SHE WAS PREGNANT. I WANTED TO KEEP YOU SCARED.
ARE YOU ALL RIGHT?
NO.
YOU MIND CALLING THE STATION FOR ME?
We didn't get out of town until after three in the morning.
I was so wired, so drained, that I didn't even pay any attention to the lightning. For the first time in a long time, it didn't bother me.
I felt so sorry for Hollis.
SHERIFF
Sarne County
SHERIFF
Sarne County
SHERIFF
Sarne County
SHERIFF
Sarne County

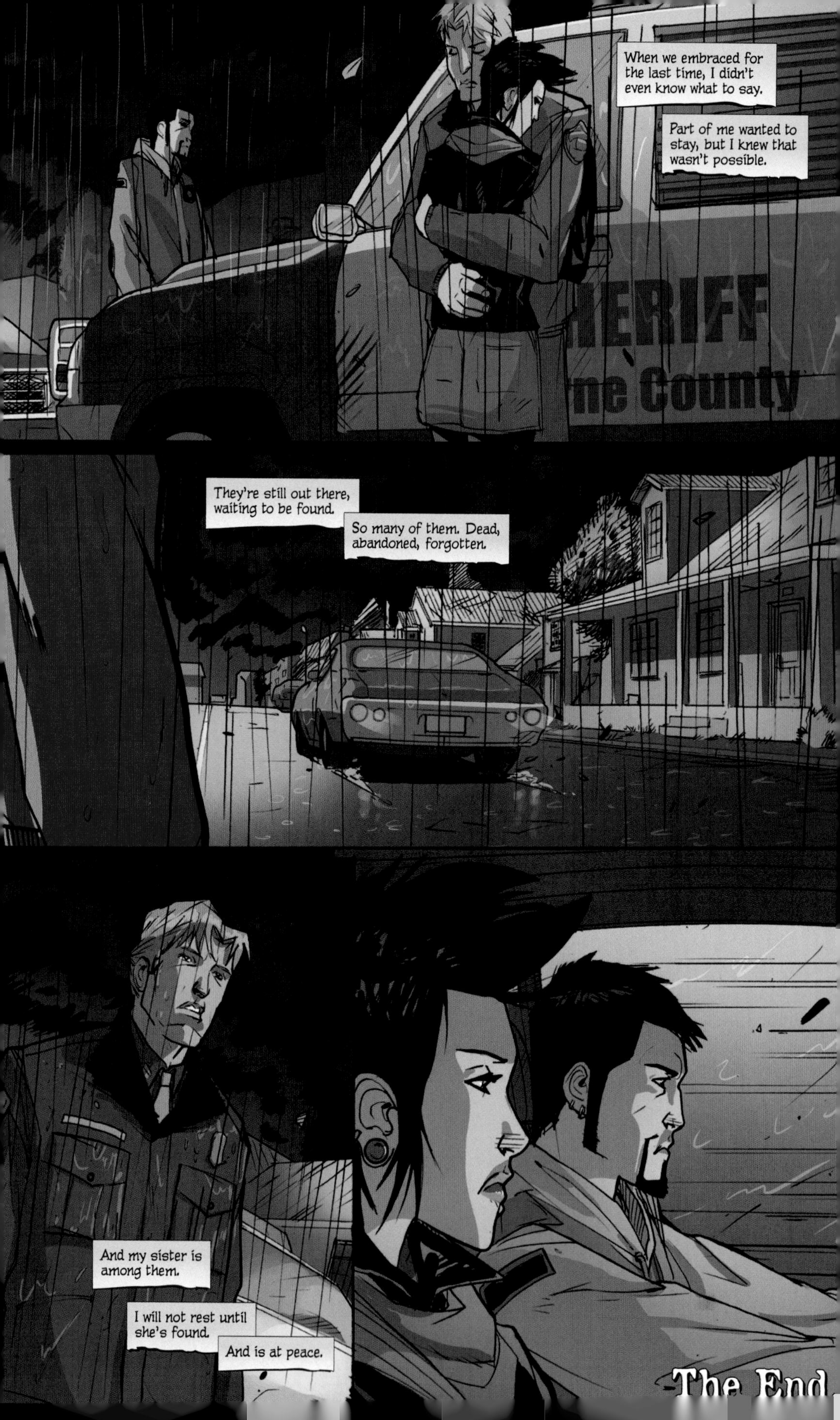
When we embraced for the last time, I didn't even know what to say.
Part of me wanted to stay, but I knew that wasn't possible.
SHERIFF
ne County
They're still out there, waiting to be found.
So many of them. Dead, abandoned, forgotten.
And my sister is among them.
I will not rest until she's found.
And is at peace.
The End

GRAVE SIGHT
BONUS MATERIAL

THE MAKING OF GRAVE SIGHT
AN INTERVIEW WITH NOVELIST CHARLAINE HARRIS

How have you enjoyed seeing Harper Connelly converted to the comics format?
It's been interesting. Sometimes I get pretty excited by what I see in the artwork, because it looks so similar to the pictures in my head. Sometimes I think, "Oh, gosh, I never thought it might have looked that way!" And that too is a pretty interesting perspective.

At this point in the Harper Connelly series, which is now the end of the first novel, how well will readers know Harper? And what should they know about what's coming up for them to discover?

I think that Harper is on her way to becoming a person who doesn't keep herself closed in, a person who connects more with the human race around her, and a person who is willing to admit the most emotional thing in her life. And I think that she also becomes a little more realistic in a lot of ways. I mean, in the books anyway, she comes to realize she can't maintain her two little half-sisters with any consistency. She comes to understand that they're well off where they are. She comes to understand that a lot of the things she's been dreaming about are going to remain dreams, but that she and Tolliver can have a life together. And I think she comes to be a little more at peace with herself.

Harper has the ability to see how and why people died…but not who killed them if they were murdered. How did you develop the parameters of her powers?

Well, it wouldn't be a very long book if she just said, "Oh, yeah, it was him!" [Laughs] It had to be something that would work in a mystery setting. And, obviously, if you can see the identity of the murderer, that makes for a very short, boring book. So I had to put a limit to it. And her connection is with the bones of the victims, so I don't think that that's a totally unreasonable limitation to put on it.

Where did the inspiration for *Grave Sight* come from?

I was wanting to write something different from the Sookie Stackhouse novels, and I wanted to write something maybe a little darker—in my view anyway. I know that some people think the Sookie ones are quite dark, but they're not, in my view. And I've always been pretty interested in lightning. No matter how often I read an explanation of why lightning happens, it still seems like magic to me. I've always been interested in stories of people who have been struck by lightning and lived to talk about it. So I joined a listserv for people who've been lightning-struck, and they were kind enough to let me lurk there for a while. I just found it really fascinating what a grab bag of consequences they suffered as a result of being struck by lightning. So my imagination began to take off from that.

Was Harper based on any real-life person you observed in that group?

No, she wasn't.

How would you compare Harper Connelly to Sookie Stackhouse?

Well, certainly Harper is a more grim personality who grew up without the love and caring that Sookie had when she grew up. Sookie grew up with a strong sense of community, and Harper didn't. Harper only had her siblings to help her, and they weren't really her siblings. Though Sookie had a very rough upbringing because of her telepathy, Harper was betrayed by everybody around her. Her parents, who should have taken the best care of her, were the ones who let her down the most.

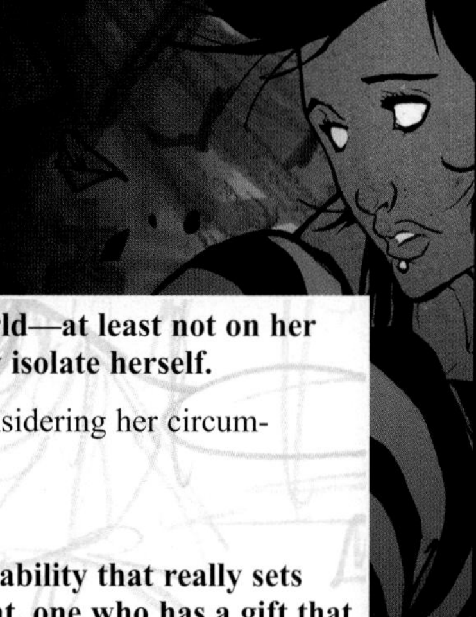

She's somewhat jaded, but she's not exactly alienated from the world—at least not on her end. Other people try to alienate her more than she tries to actively isolate herself.

I would agree. I think that she's made a very successful adaptation, considering her circumstances.

Both Harper and Sookie are similar in that they have this singular ability that really sets them apart. Is there something about crafting a heroine such as that, one who has a gift that seems enviable at first, that makes you identify with them as a writer?

Maybe that's a result of growing up as a writer in a society that didn't really believe I could do any such thing. [Laughs]

But you proved them wrong.

Yeah, I did, but sometimes that's kind of a hollow victory, when you had a pretty intense teenagerdom to live through first. [Laughs]

Are some of your life experiences mirrored in those of your characters?

Not literally, but maybe figuratively, yes. Maybe in essence the feelings are the same, but the circumstances are different.

Did you have any influence over the art on the book and how artist Denis Medri depicted any scenes?

I get all the artwork first when it's been "roughed in" and then when it's been colored and lettered. Seeing something in the various stages of development is really interesting for me. I feel like I'm learning a little bit about the business.

Have any scenes from the comic book really struck you as interesting, especially when compared to how you wrote them in the prose books?

Well, I think the scene where Harper and Tolliver are talking to one of Teenie's possible fathers, and he's sitting on the front porch of his wife's house after she's been murdered—there's something about that that really struck me. He looks so shifty. You can tell he's done something wrong. I just thought that was a very striking scene.

You wrote four Harper Connelly novels. Do you have any plans to go back to the series at this point?

I don't believe I will, because I'm usually pretty set on walking away when I feel like I've said everything about a character I have to say. And I'm pretty sure I've said everything about Harper that I have to say. Though something else might occur to me.

Did you enjoy developing her character and writing about her?

Absolutely. She's a very interesting person and quite a bit different from anybody I've ever written before. So it was kind of a challenge to represent her fully.

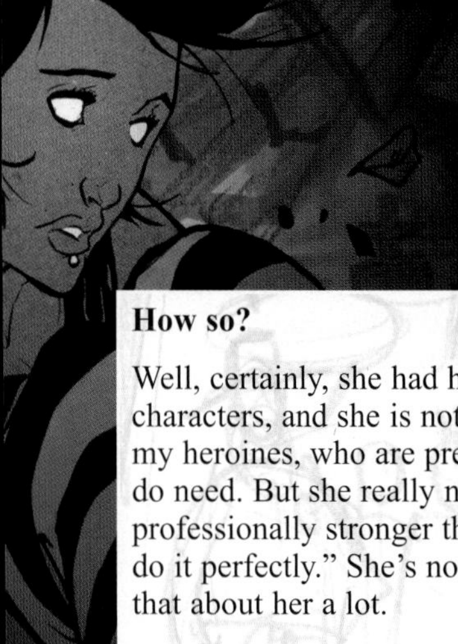

How so?

Well, certainly, she had had a super-difficult upbringing, I think more so than any of my other characters, and she is not afraid to admit that she needs other people, which is not the norm for my heroines, who are pretty independent or at least never think too much about the people they do need. But she really needs Tolliver, and she's not afraid to admit it. At the same time, she is professionally stronger than any of my other protagonists. She says, you know, "I do my job and I do it perfectly." She's not afraid of death or afraid of her expertise, her own strong points. I like that about her a lot.

Her confidence in her work is kind of in stark contrast to how other people view her job. Even the people who hire her are often angry at her for it, and the fact that she charges money to tell people how their loved ones died. Is what she's doing a positive thing, in your mind, or is it controversial?

I don't know if I consider it controversial or not. I consider her a true survivor who's making her living in the only way she can think of to do so. She's essentially turning a disability into an asset by earning her living, and Tolliver's, by exploiting the consequences of the terrible thing that happened to her. It's really a case of making lemonade from lemons, I think. And I thought that was kind of admirable, myself.

Speaking of Tolliver, her stepbrother, one of the interesting facets about the books is her relationship with him, which grows over the books. What do you think of how the comic portrays their relationship at this point?

I think it's absolutely like it was in the books. I'm really delighted to see that they're adhering to the story line in the books so closely and picking up all the essential markers that are leading to their eventual rapprochement.

Was Tolliver a character you enjoyed developing and writing?

Yes. He's not as clear to me as Harper is, but I think he finds happiness, too. He finds out more about his family and he comes to understand that they've been living a lie in a lot of ways, which is sad, but it's better to know than to not know.

The *Grave Sight* comics are structured and paced a little differently than the prose books. How did you feel about the different set-up of the comic?

Well, certainly after all my experiences, I know that different mediums require different structures. I've certainly seen that in the *True Blood* television series, and it doesn't surprise me at all that the comic book series would need to be told in a different way.

Were there any scenes from the prose book that you were disappointed weren't able to make it into the comic adaptation?

I try not to second-guess the artist, the same way I've made my peace with the television show. Not everything from the books could be adapted—not every point I loved or felt was especially well done could be brought into the pared-down medium of the comic book. And the same thing with the TV show, which of course is very different from the original work. I guess I've really adjusted to the fact that, if you translate my work into something different, there are going to be additions and subtractions.

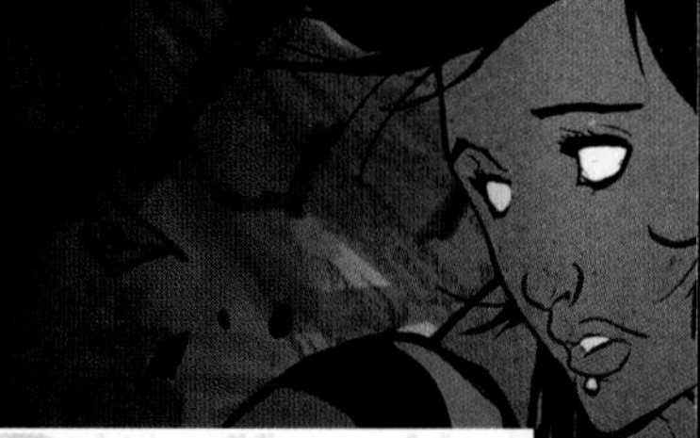

A lot of your fans aren't always so calm about those changes.

Oh, yeah! Oh, yeah. I hear about it a lot. And honestly, I hope that they like the TV show, too, because I think it's a fun show. I enjoy watching it. But at the same time, if they don't, that's okay, too. It's not the books. I don't take it personally if they don't like it. I just hope that people will always enjoy the books as well as the TV show, just as with the Harper Connelly books I hope that people will enjoy the comic books and again will pick up the novels and read them.

Were you a fan of comics before doing this?

I did read them as a child. I loved Archie! In latter years, I haven't been such a fan of them. But I'm seeing that the art is really extraordinary now.

In addition to working on this, you're doing another graphic novel, called *Cemetery Girl*, with writer Christopher Golden. What can you reveal about that?

It'll be released next year. It's about a young woman who gets dumped in a cemetery. She's completely lost her memory and she doesn't know why she's there or where she came from. She doesn't know her name. But she does know, of course, that someone is trying to kill her. In fact, she actually dies for a minute and comes back. She's quite young, in her teens, and she starts living in the cemetery. She finds a crypt and lines it with the fake grass they cover the mounds with. She starts developing her whole life in this cemetery because she's afraid to come out into the open since she doesn't know who's trying to kill her.

Has working on *Cemetery Girl* affected how you look at the comic-book adaptations of your work?

Well, of course I'm looking at the comic books in a much smarter way now that I'm learning how they're being put together, and I'm chiding myself for my ignorance. When they send me the rough sketches, I had been looking at them going, "I can't really make sense out of these. I don't know why they show them to me!" But now I'm getting it a lot more and I'm studying the way the panels are put together, and the lettering. And how they pick the right words for the characters to say. And I'm trying to learn from looking at the process of producing the Harper comic books with a view to making *Cemetery Girl* better.

There has been talk that the Harper Connelly books would be turned into a CBS series. Has that moved forward?

That's pretty much in a coma.

Would you like to see it adapted to TV?

Yes, I would, but I feel like I've had the Cadillac of TV experiences, so it would be really hard to match that again.

Do you interact much with Alan Ball about what happens on *True Blood*? Does he run things by you?

It's pretty much separate. If I hadn't trusted Alan, I wouldn't have signed the books over to him, because I had other offers I passed up. So Alan is doing his own thing and I respect that. I admire his talent.

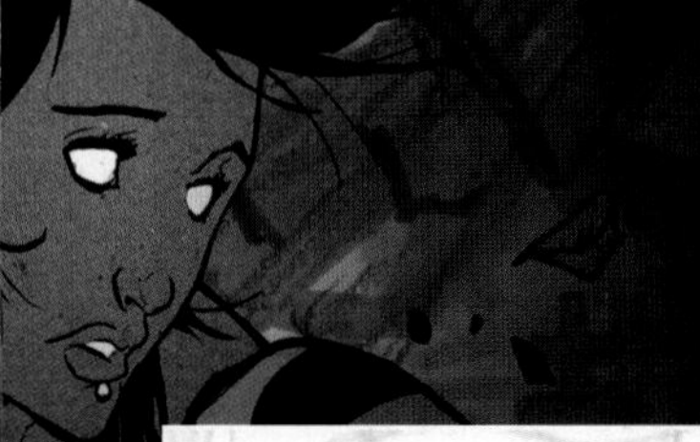

Like the Sookie Stackhouse books, *Grave Sight* is set in the south. Do you think the supernatural stories you write are better suited to the south?

Well, I have a couple of thoughts about that. Of course, I am southern and I write with a southern accent. But I think the supernatural is universal. I've read ghost stories set in Maine that were just as good as ghost stories set in New Orleans. Or California, for that matter. I think the supernatural is with us in every part of the United States. It's just a little prettier when it's got Spanish moss on it.

What first drove your interest in the supernatural?

Isn't everybody interested in the supernatural? Most people want to believe that there is something beyond what we can see and hear and smell. They want to believe there's more.

I would imagine that writing about these types of things allows you to hear some interesting supernatural stories from your readers.

You would think, wouldn't you? But I haven't heard anything that extraordinary. I am *ready* to hear! Bring it on!

Charlaine Harris is a *New York Times* bestselling author who has been writing for thirty years. She was born and raised in the Mississippi River Delta area. She is also the author of the successful Sookie Stackhouse urban fantasy series about a telepathic waitress named Sookie Stackhouse who works in a bar in the fictional Northern Louisiana town of Bon Temps. Sookie Stackhouse has proven to be so popular that it has been adapted into *True Blood* for HBO. It was an instant success and is now filming its fifth season. Harris is married and the mother of three and lives in Texas.

COVERING **GRAVE SIGHT**

A LOOK AT THE COVERS FOR GRAVE SIGHT ONE THROUGH THREE

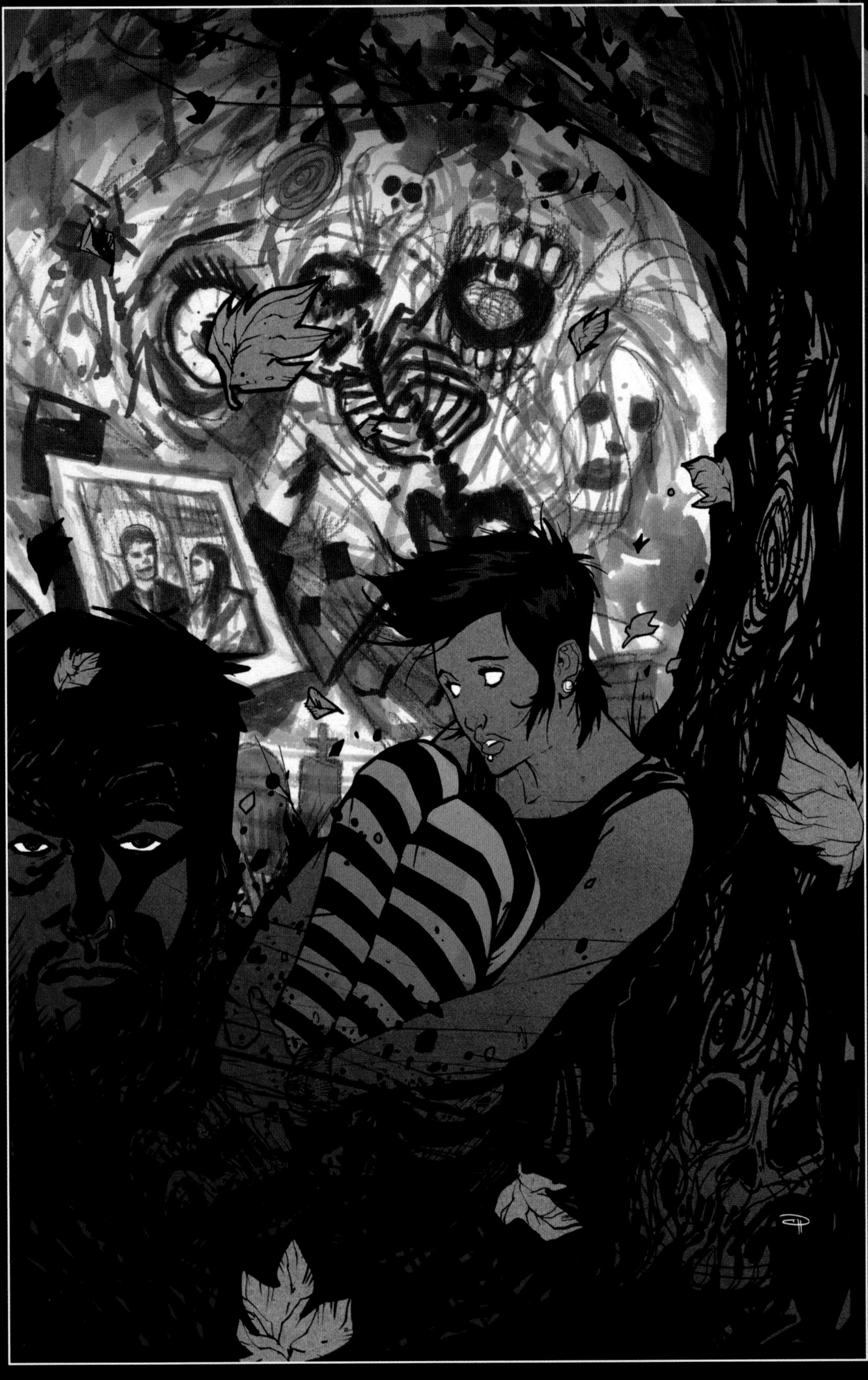

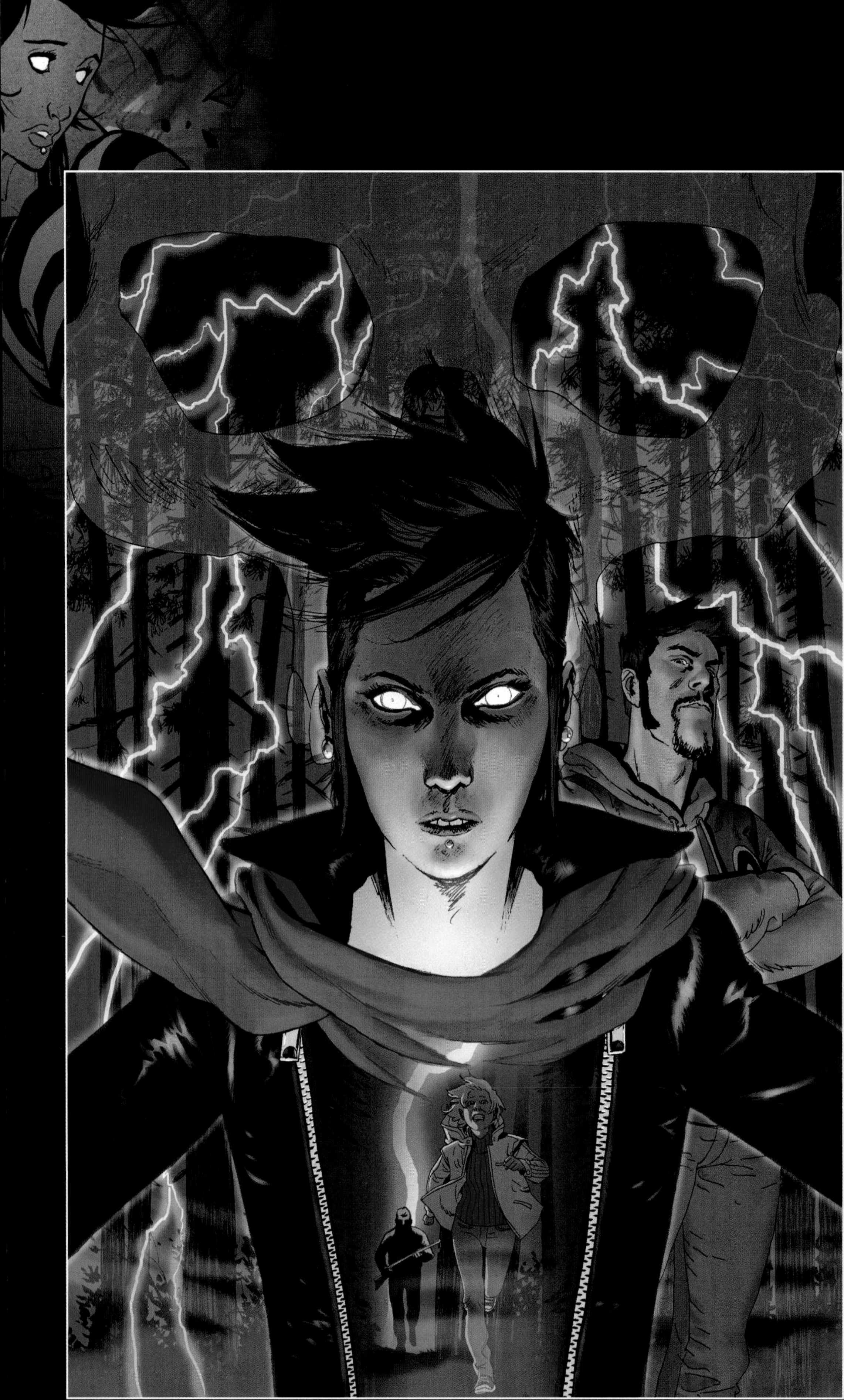

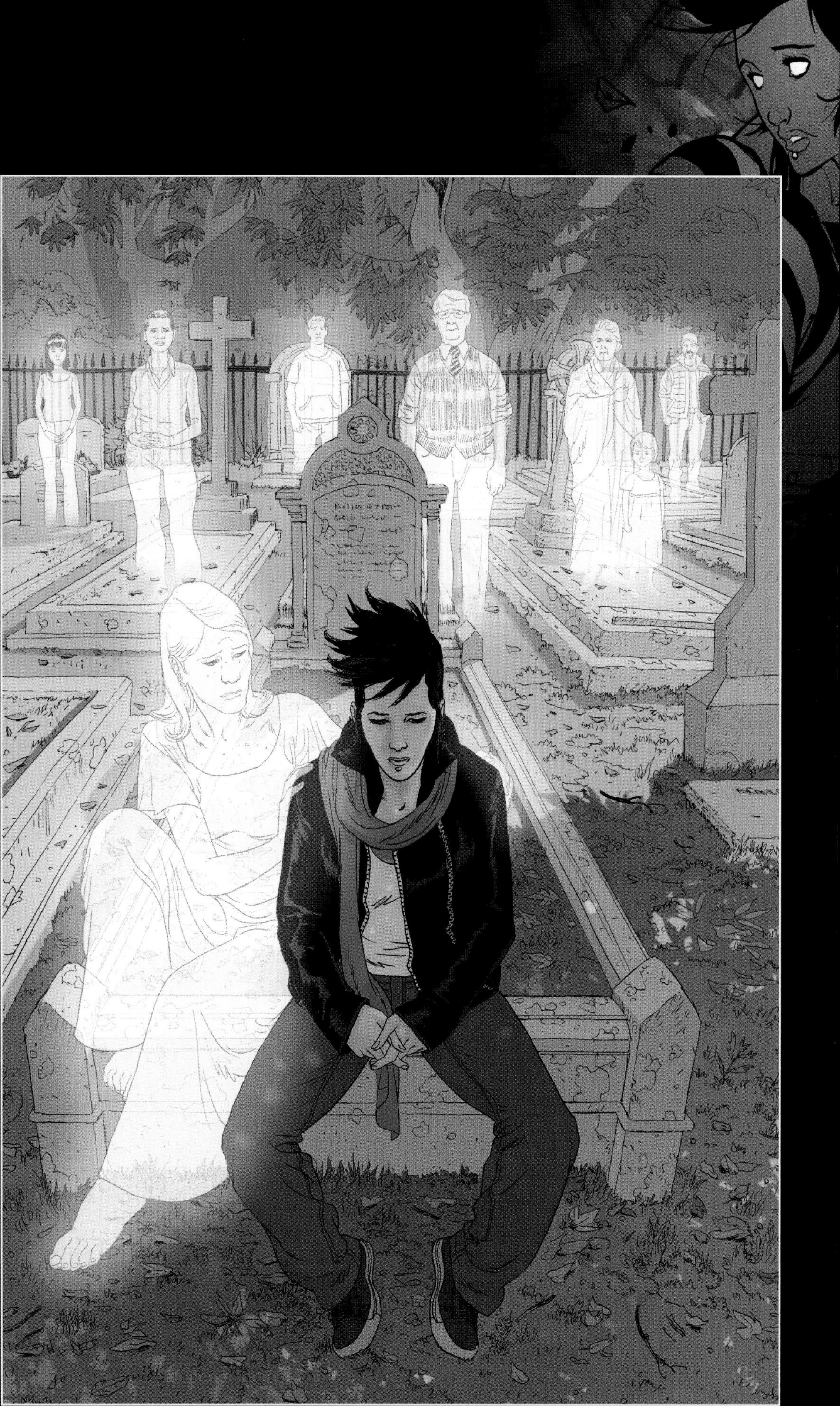

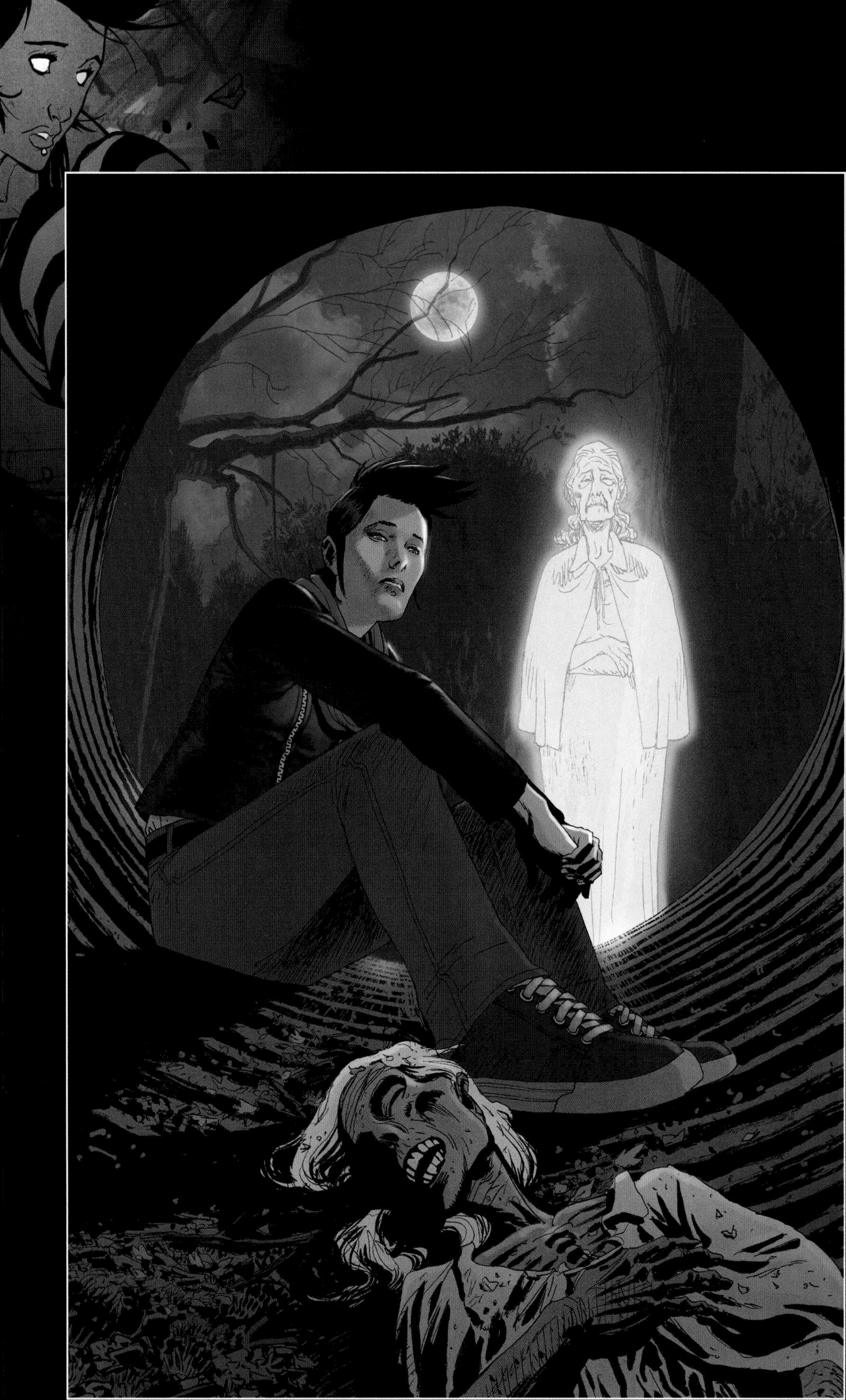

THE MAKING OF GRAVE SIGHT

THE ORIGINAL SIX-PART SERIES PITCH BY WILLIAM HARM

General Notes:

Like the novel, the comic book version of *Grave Sight* will be narrated (via captions) by Harper. However, because of the visual nature of the comic book medium, the narration won't be as extensive. In addition, the focus will occasionally shift to other characters, like Tolliver (when he's in jail), to better utilize the medium.

When Harper uses her "ability", this will be shown visually and be a little more extensive than it is in the novel. When Harper "sees" what happens to Teenie, for example, this will extend across multiple pages — the reader will watch Teenie run through the woods, desperately trying to escape, crying that Dell is dead, all before getting shot in the back.

The disappearance of Cameron will play a larger role in the story, with Harper carrying around a folder that contains all of the news clippings on her sister's disappearance. Harper's obsessed with finding out what happened to her sister, and it tears her up inside that she can find so many other dead people, but she can't find out what happened to Cameron.

The incident in Montana will be shown to the reader (it'll open the series). This is a great way of visually showing how people feel about Harper — and it also makes Tolliver's arrest seem less random since the reader will be familiar with the incident.

I'd also like to insert a couple new scenes that show Harper using her abilities in other settings. Since she doesn't use her abilities much in the last half of the book (except when Anderson shoots at her), I want to make sure the reader is always thinking about how strange and wonderful this woman is, how her gift dictates her entire life.

(Perhaps one of the scenes is of her trying to be "normal", at a park or something, and the dead just won't shut up.)

Several scenes will be condensed/edited for space reasons. For example, when Harper and Tolliver initially go out to locate Teenie's body, Hollis is already with them. The essential parts of the mystery will always be maintained.

Helen's murder will be shown in real-time, although the identity of the killer will remain a complete secret. Again, this will help visual the story and take advantage of the medium.

Issue-by-Issue Breakdown:

<u>ISSUE ONE:</u>

Flashback: Open in Montana, the people trying to stone Harper. Total chaos. Tolliver intervenes and is arrested.

The present: Harper and Tolliver have just come from their first meeting with the townspeople, and Harper's pissed. She finds Mr. Chesswood's body and calls the sheriff. After confirming the body's where Harper says it is, she's hired.

The next morning. Edwards, Tolliver, Harper, and Hollis are on the road near where Dell's body was found. Harper and Tolliver head into the woods, find the body of the hunter and then find Teenie's body.

Hollis confirms the existence of the body. Harper and Tolliver return to the hotel, and Tolliver heads out to try and score with the waitress.

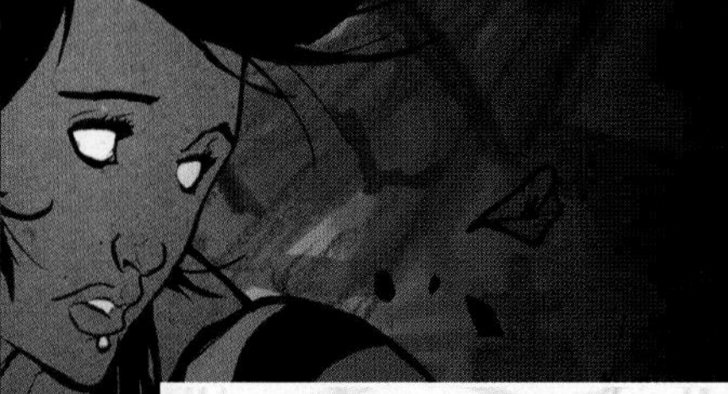

Harper reviews the materials that she has on Cameron.

Hollis comes to the hotel and he and Harper go out. He hires Harper, who tells him that Sally was murdered.

ISSUE TWO:

Hollis takes Harper back to the hotel (she leaves the money on his seat). The storm hits and Tolliver takes care of her.

Harper and Tolliver visit Helen, and then leave for the next job.

Helen is murdered.

Harper stands in the cemetery with Mrs. Roller. She tells Mrs. Roller that he husband was killed by the cat. Roller freaks out just as Tolliver arrives from cashing the check. Harper gets into the car and Tolliver tells her that they have to return to Sarne.

Sheriff Branscom interviews Harper. (The bit about her charging Hollis is mentioned here.)

Hollis interviews Tolliver. As they leave, Harper goes off on Holliver for lying about the money.

Mary Nell and the others come to the hotel. After they leave, Tolliver and Harper make their plans to head for Memphis.

ISSUE THREE:

Flashback: A distraught Harper walking down the street, desperately trying to get a reading on Cameron, trying to find out what happened to her. She collapses and weeps.

The present: Harper and Tolliver are the cemetery so that Harper can practice. Hollis comes out and tells them they need to go to the station.

The state police question Harper (and Tolliver) about Helen's murder. On the way out, they're harassed by Scott and the others. They make plans to have dinner with Mary Nell.

At dinner, Mary Nell tells them that Teenie was pregnant with Dell's child. Later, Harper goes out with Hollis.

The next morning, Harper maces Scott the other boys. She then goes to the funeral home and speaks with Annie.

Harper attends the concert with Hollis. They sleep together.

ISSUE FOUR:

Harper and Tolliver conduct research at the newspaper, and then the two of them visit Sybil's house.

As they drive to meet Jay, they get a call about Mariella. They meet with Jay, and then Tolliver's arrested as they mail the DNA samples.

Harper calls Art and then talks with Hollis. After calling Phyllis, Harper goes for a run and breaks

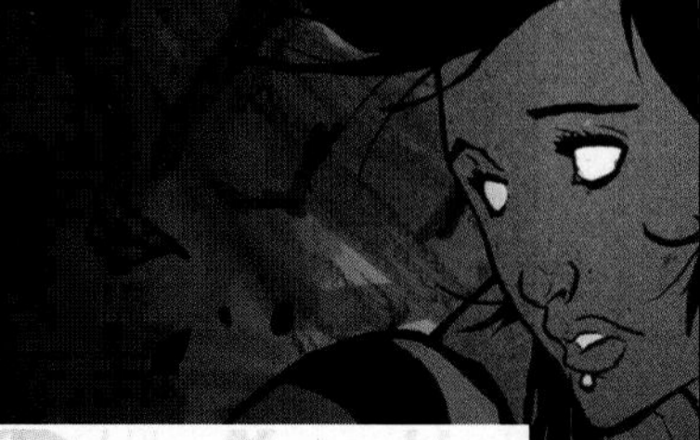

into Hollis' house. She's caught, they have sex again, and the discuss what Sally was looking for.

Hollis takes Harper back to her hotel room, and as she enters, she's brutally attacked by a shadowed figure.

ISSUE FIVE:

Flashback: Harper helps an elderly man discover what happened to his younger brother. The man is so happy, he kisses Harper over and over on the cheeks. She has a gift from God, he says. (I want to show that some people appreciate what Harper does.)

The present: Harper fights Scot, who's then arrested by Hollis. Harper fights with the owner of the hotel and then goes into her room where she looks at the letters (SO MO DA NO) and Cameron's case file.

The next morning. Tolliver takes verbal abuse at the jail, but refuses to get angry, start a fight.

Harper tries to visit Tolliver, is turned away, so she goes to the Teague family plot where she's shot at. She calls the police; Bledsoe arrives and she leaves.

Harper visits Tolliver in jail and then talks with Mary Nell.

Tolliver appears before the judge and is released.

ISSUE SIX:

Tolliver's released from jail, and he and Harper make plans to leave. They end up being trapped by the impending storm, so they decide to get dinner.

During dinner, Sybil calls and tells them that they need to come to her house. Harper also figures out the meaning of Dick Teague's message.

They arrive at Sybil's, and it's revealed that Paul murdered Dell, Teenie, and Helen. Sybil murdered Sally.

After everyone's arrested, Hollis says his goodbyes to Harper and Tolliver, who then leave town for good.

William Harms has been a professional writer and editor for nearly 15 years. His comic book work has been published by Marvel Comics, DC Comics, Image Comics, and Top Cow, among others.

A finalist for the prestigious International Horror Guild Award -- one of the top literary awards for horror and dark fantasy -- William's comic and video game writing has received accolades from a wide variety of sources, including *The Daily Telegraph, USA Today, San Francisco Chronicle, Aint-it-Cool News, IGN Comics*, and *Fangoria*.

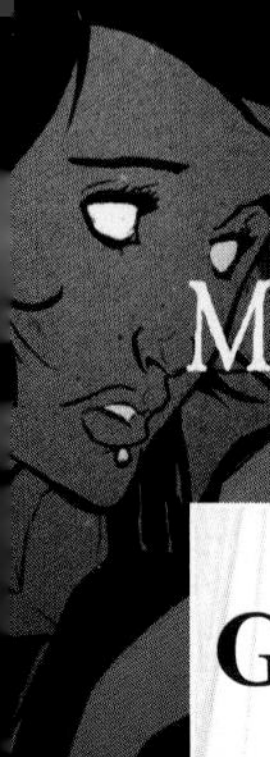

THE MAKING OF GRAVE SIGHT

TWO-PAGE TRY-OUT SCRIPT AND ART BY WILLIAM AND DENIS

Grave Sight: Sample Script:

This is the scene where Harper finds Teenie's body. It'll be integrated into the full script for ISSUE 1.

PAGE 1

PANEL 1: Harper and Tolliver move through the woods, Harper leading the way. She's wearing large, dark sunglasses, a red scarf, blue padded jacket, gloves, and hiking boots. Tolliver's dressed in the same type of clothing — they were ready to come out into the woods. Her hands are at her sides, as if she's "feeling" for something. They're climbing up a small hill.

This is the Ozarks, so the ground should be covered with leaves, trees are everywhere, and here and there the bald faces of rocks are exposed, jutting up out of the ground.

TOLLIVER: You feel something?

HARPER: Yeah. This way.

PANEL 2: They continue up the hill, walking silently, Harper "feeling" her way.

PANEL 3: Still on the hill. The area's clear of trees, and Harper's kneeling down, hands hovering above a pile of dry, dead branches and leaves.

PANEL 4: Tight on Harper's eyes. We see them through the glasses — her eyes have gone totally white, are wide open as she experiences the last moments of Teenie's life.

PANEL 5: Same, but now Harper's eyes are morphing into a new scene: Teenie (teenager, pretty but poor) running through the woods at night.

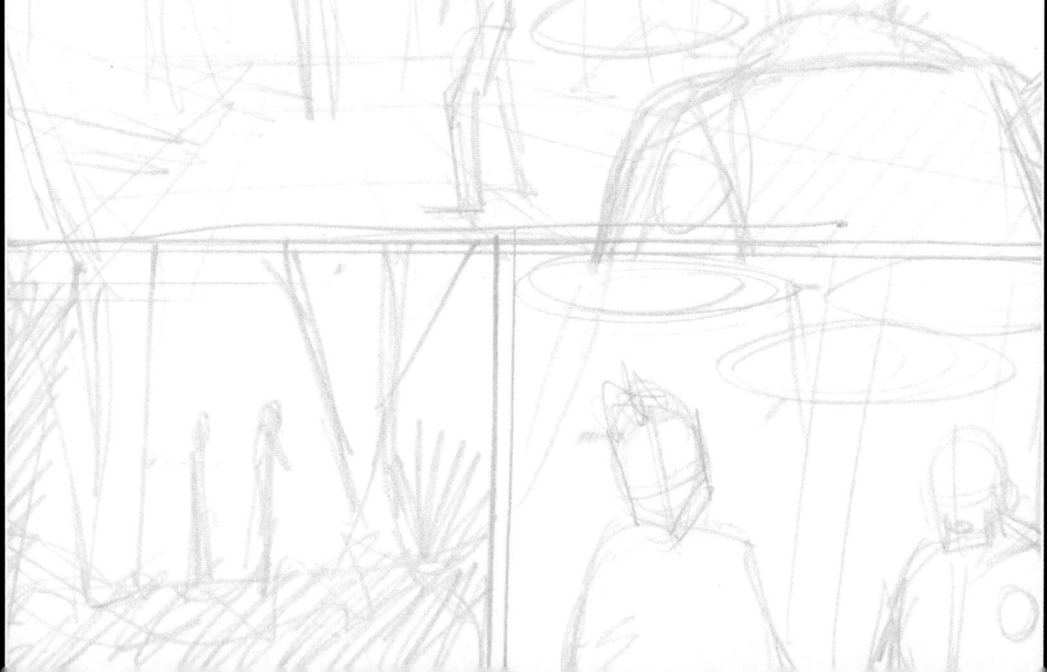

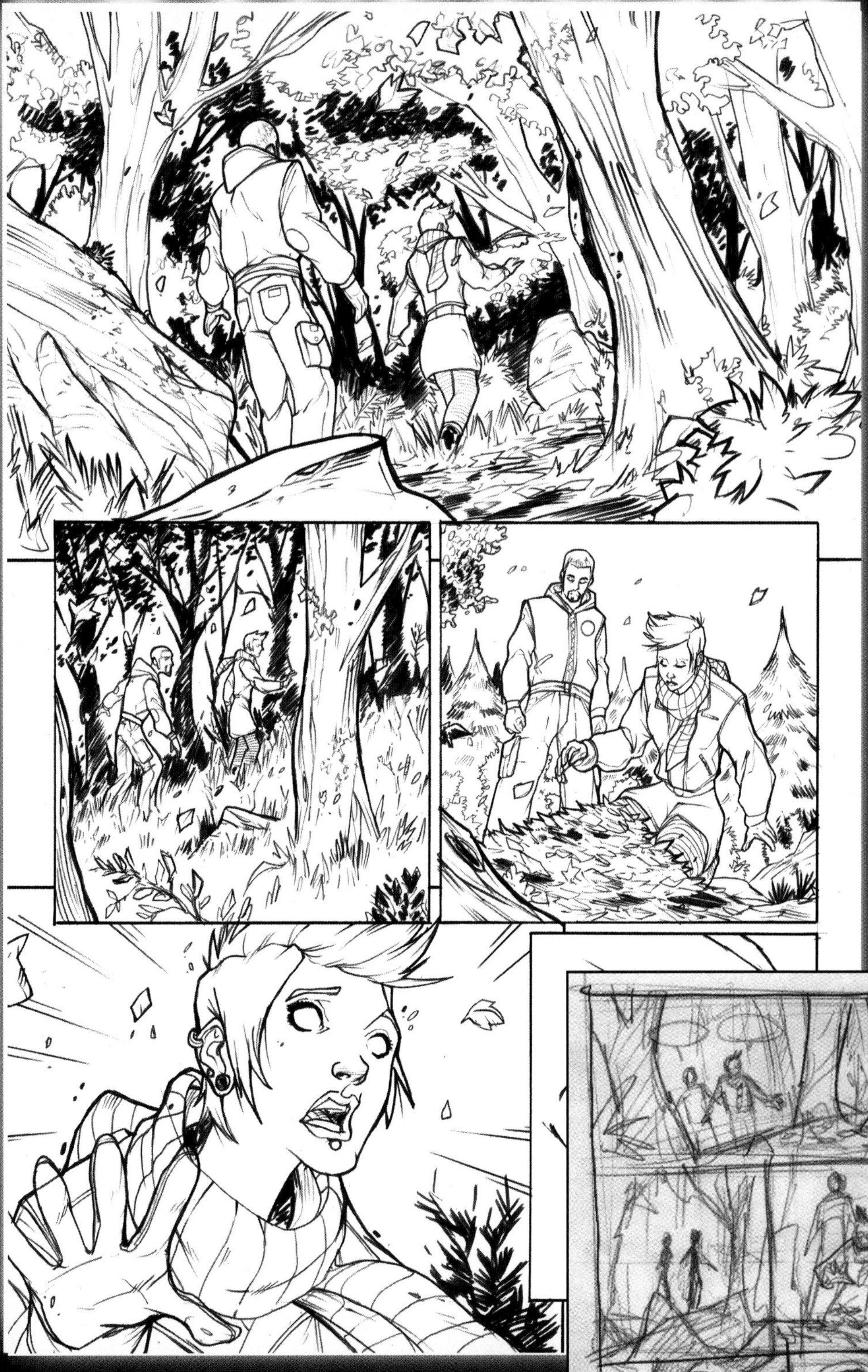

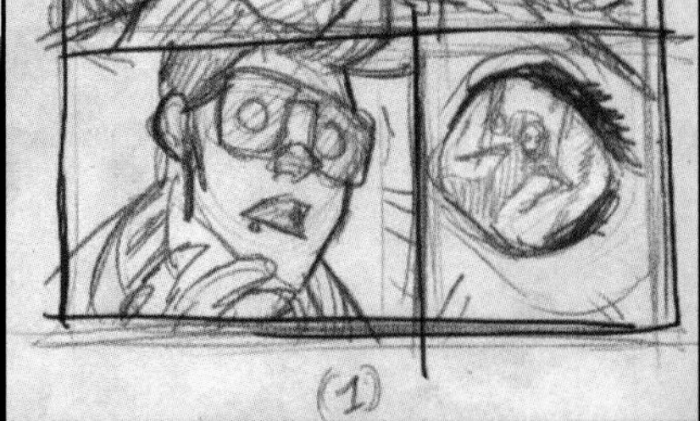

Top: final try-out art by DENIS MEDRI
Bottom: rough layout by DENIS MEDRI

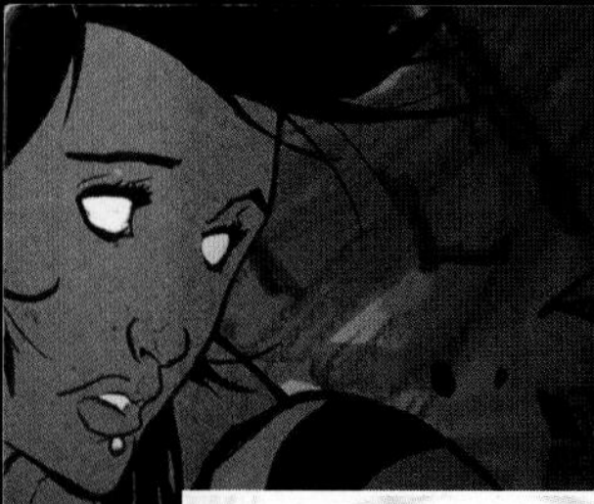

Grave Sight: Sample Script:

PAGE TWO

PANEL 1: We're now "seeing" the last moments of Teenie's life the same way Harper's seeing it, through her powers. This is a weird flashback, everything angled and exaggerated. Teenie continues to run, starting up the same hill, panting and terrified.

TEENIE (weird, dream-like): …oh God…

PANEL 2: Tight on Teenie. She looks back over her should, scared out of his mind.

TEENIE (weird, dream-like): …please, leave me alone…

PANEL 3: Teenie struggles up the hill, trying to run but having a hard time getting traction, keeping her balance.

PANEL 4: Wide panel. Teenie, small in the panel, is shot in the back.

SFX: BLAM

PANEL 5: Teenie on her stomach, hands dug into the cold earth. Blood pooling out from her mouth, from the wound in her back. She's dying.

PANEL 6: On the ground, near Teenie's face, looking up. A shadowed figure stands behind her, gun pointed down. The gun fires, once again striking her in the back.

SFX: BLAM

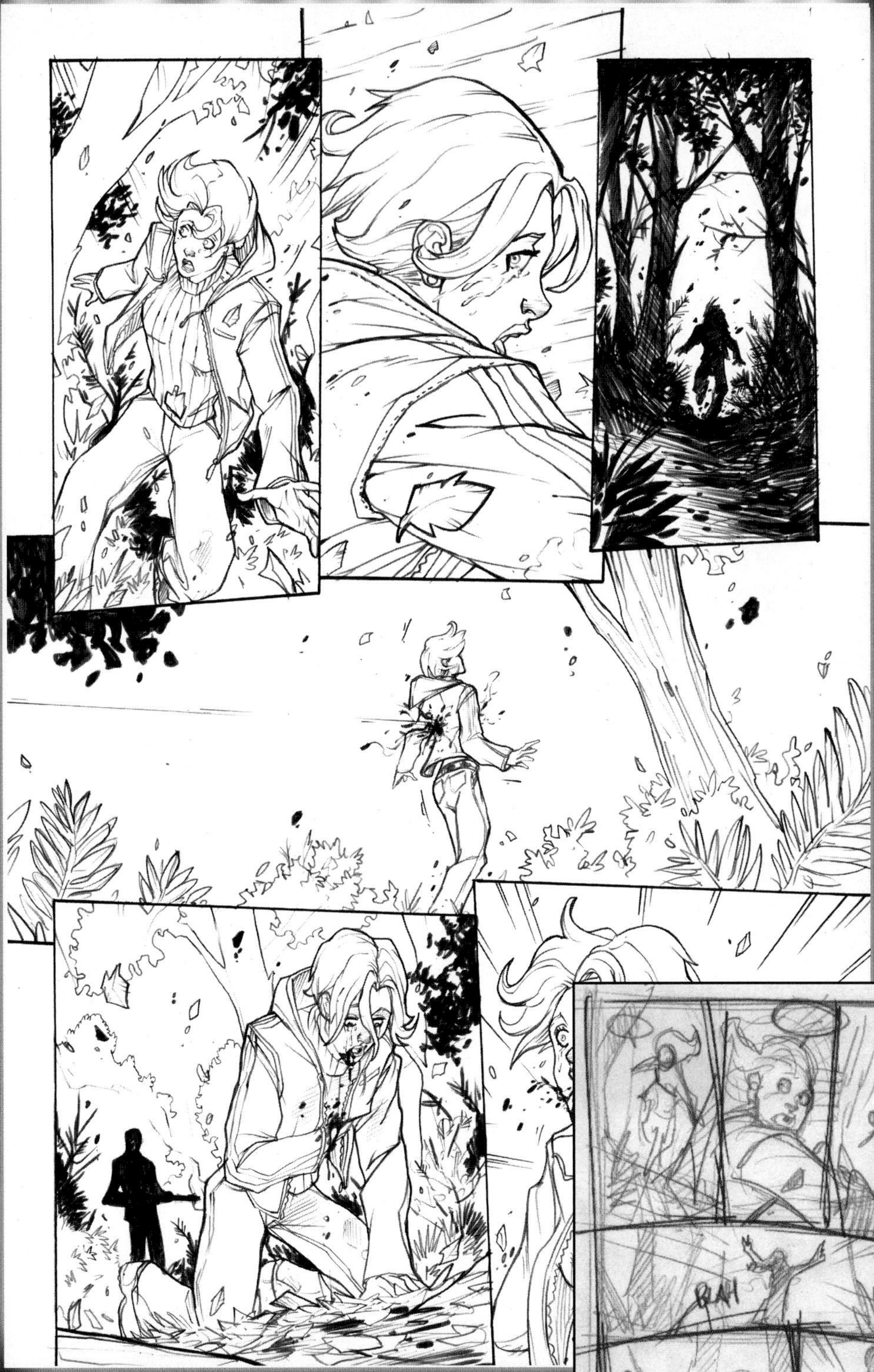

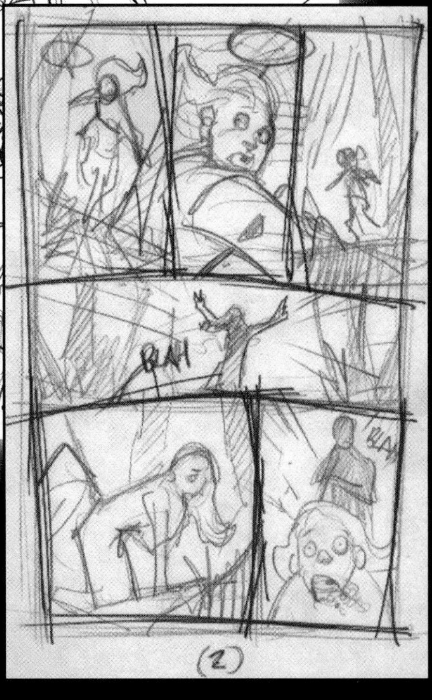
(2)

Top: final try-out art by DENIS MEDRI
Bottom: rough layout by DENIS MEDRI

THE CAST OF GRAVE SIGHT

A LOOK AT WILLIAM'S BREAKDOWN OF THE MAIN CHARACTERS

HARPER CONNELLY

Twenty-four years old, five foot seven, black hair. Runs a lot, so she's in good shape, but she's a little on the thin side. Kind of mousey, but still pretty. Doesn't spend a lot of time on her appearance.

Her right leg was permanently injured when she was struck by lightning, and because of this it's weaker than her left leg and scarred with a spider web-like pattern.

TOLLIVER LANG

Twenty-eight years old, six feet tall, black hair with a reddish mustache. He has scars on his face from acne and wide, slightly boney shoulders. Despite his acne scars, he's quite a ladies man and exudes confidence.

HOLLIS BOXLEITNER

Husky, crooked nose, broad face. Pale blond hair. He ends up being Harper's love interest, so he should be handsome in a sort-of traditional way.

SHERIFF HARVEY BRANSCOM

Mid-fifties, white hair and mustache, reddish face. I picture him as being slightly overweight. Not the stereotypical Southern sheriff, but the job's taken a toll.

PAUL EDWARDS

Tanned, good looking, early forties. Clean-shaven. He relies on his looks to get by in life.

SYBIL TEAGUE

Early forties, pretty in a *Real Housewives of New York City* kind of way. Takes pride in her appearance. She's rich and her clothing makes that obvious to everyone who sees her.

MARY NELL TEAGUE

Sybil's daughter. Teenager who wears a lot of make-up and tight clothes. She's naturally pretty, but she tries too hard.

TERENCE "TERRY" VALE

The mayor. Round face, nearly bald. Just a few stray hairs combed in a desperate manner. Wears wire-rimmed glasses.